Preschool Art

18561   649.5

D1078008

Preschool

ART

It's the process, not the product

By MaryAnn Kohl

Illustrations by K. Whelan Dery

Brilliant Publications

Dedication

In memory of my grandmother, Mary Geanne Faubion Wilson, the first published author I ever knew, who sparked my imagination when she told me that angels made my freckles when they kissed me on the nose as I slept.

Acknowledgements

I would like to thank my editor, Kathy Charner, for her ability to organize my writing schedule for *Preschool Art* and also her humour and kindness in our editor–author relationship. Sometimes I think we were just having too much fun to call this work! I would like to thank the owners of Gryphon House, Leah and Larry Rood, for their support and friendship, and their belief in this book and in me. Most important, my thanks go to my husband, Michael, and my daughters, Hannah and Megan, who keep my mind clear, tell me when I've been wonderful or when I haven't and remind me of what is most important in life.

Originally published by Gryphon House, Inc.
10726 Tucker Street, Beltsville, MD 20705, USA

Published in the UK by Brilliant Publications,
The Old School Yard, Leighton Road, Northall,
Dunstable, Bedfordshire LU6 2HA

Written by MaryAnn Kohl
Illustrated by K. Whelan Dery
Cover photograph by Martyn Chillmaid

© 1994 MaryAnn Kohl
ISBN 1 897675 49 6

First published in the UK in 1999
10 9 8 7 6 5 4 3 2 1

Printed and bound in Malta by Interprint Limited

The right of MaryAnn Kohl to be identified as the author of this work has been asserted by her in accordance with the Copyright, Designs and Patents Act 1988.

A special note about process art

Dear Fellow Artists,

Welcome to the world of process art, a world you already know quite well if you have ever scribbled with crayons on paper just to see the colours mix and swirl! Do you like smearing your hand through cool, smooth fingerpaint and watching colours mix on the paper? Do you enjoy finding interesting collage materials and gluing them on silver foil? Then you will love *Preschool Art*! It is filled with months of art experiences for every child, aged three to six (and older brothers and sisters, mums, dads and grandparents, too), to explore.

"Process, not product" means that you can explore art materials and enjoy what happens. You don't have to copy what an adult makes or even try to make something a friend has made. There is no right or wrong way for these art ideas to turn out; there is only YOUR way. YOU are the artist.

Have you ever spread cool, smooth fingerpaint across a baking tray? Well, you should try it … it feels wonderful and the most exciting things happen to the paint. I won't tell you what because I don't want to spoil the surprise of the process of art. When you try fingerpainting on a baking tray, don't concern yourself with what you should make. Just enjoy the doing. That's the whole idea of process art.

Have you ever melted crayons on a warming tray? This book tells you how to get started, and the process will amaze you! Some very strange and wonderful things happen to crayon when it is liquid. I know you'll enjoy the creative process of discovering just what happens!

Oh, I almost forgot to tell you something important! It's perfectly all right if you don't want to save whatever art experience you just finished. You can throw it away or take it home or cut it up into little pieces and glue them on something else. Simply enjoy creating.

I hope you have a wonderful time with the process of art as you discover, create and explore your way through a whole year full of art experiences. Oh, and don't forget to help clean up!

Process, not product!

Mary Ann Kohl

ps This page may be photocopied.

Using the icons

Each activity has up to five icons to make the project in *Preschool Art* more usable and accessible for the artist, care-giver, teacher or parent. These icons are suggestions, subject to your personal and individual modifications or changes based on your experience and needs. Experiment with materials, vary suggested techniques or modify projects to suit the needs and abilities of each artist or each adult. Creative variation is part of the fun of providing early years art experiences.

 ### Age

Age indicates the general age range where a child can create and explore independently, that is, without much adult assistance. The "& UP" means that children this age and all ages older should be comfortable doing the project. However, children younger than the age suggested can also do the project with adult assistance. Children do not always fit the standard developmental expectations of a particular age, so decide which projects suit individual children, and their specific abilities and needs.

Planning/preparation

This icon indicates the degree of planning or preparation time an adult will need to collect materials, set up the activity or supervise the activity. Icons shown indicate planning and preparation time that is easy, moderate or involved.

 ### Help

The help icon indicates that the artist may need extra assistance from another child or from an adult during this activity.

 ### Caution

This icon appears for all activities that suggest the use of sharp, hot or electrical materials. All activities require supervision, but activities with the caution icon need extra care. For steps an adult should perform, the word "adult" is in bold type.

 ### Author's favourite

MaryAnn Kohl's favourite projects are shown with a star. Favourites are selected on the basis on one of three criteria: 1) extra fun, 2) extra fascinating or 3) extra easy and creative.

Table of Contents

Title	Page	Medium	Age	Prep 1	Prep 2	Prep 3	Help	Caution	Author
Puzzle paste	72	Craft	5	●					
Finger puppets	73	Craft	5		●		●		
Paper strip sculpture	74	Construction	5	●					

October

Title	Page	Medium	Age	Prep 1	Prep 2	Prep 3	Help	Caution	Author
Dark sugar chalk	75	Drawing	3	●					●
Handful scribble	76	Drawing	3	●					
Sponge chalk	77	Drawing	3	●					●
Spiders' web	78	Drawing	4		●		●		
Buttermilk chalk screen	79	Drawing	4			●	●		
Mystery paint	80	Painting	3	●					
Fingerprints	81	Painting	3	●					●
Tilt prints	82	Painting	3	●					●
Chalk paint	83	Painting	3	●			●		
Shoe polish leaves	84	Painting	4	●					●
Cheesy-pumpkin	85	Dough	3		●		●		
Pumpkin face mystery	86	Collage	4			●	●		
Impress wall pot	87	Craft	3			●	●	●	
Weaving board	88	Craft	4		●		●	●	
Stocking mask	89	Craft	5		●		●		
Ghost tree	90	Craft	5		●		●		
Harvest art	91	Craft	5		●		●		
Big spooky house	92	Construction	4			●	●	●	●
Peeky panel	93	Construction	5			●	●	●	●

November

Title	Page	Medium	Age	Prep 1	Prep 2	Prep 3	Help	Caution	Author
Crayon hands	94	Drawing	3	●			●		
Candle crayons	95	Drawing	3	●					
Fuzzy glue drawing	96	Drawing	3		●		●		
Transparent crayon	97	Drawing	3	●					
Dot dots	98	Drawing	4	●					
Corn-cob print	99	Painting	3		●				
Negative space	100	Painting	3		●		●		
Fingerpaint monoprint	101	Painting	3		●		●		●

Title	Page	Medium	Age	Prep 1	Prep 2	Prep 3	Help	Caution	Author
Twist and shout	102	Painting	3	●					
Palette paint	103	Painting	5		●				
String thing	104	Sculpture	4		●		●	●	
Stamped foil sculpture	105	Sculpture	4	●					●
Painted foil sculpture	106	Sculpture	4		●				
Tray punch and sew	107	Craft	3		●		●	●	
Masterpiece collection	108	Craft	3		●		●		
Cuff finger puppets	109	Craft	4		●		●		
Easy store puppet stage	110	Craft	4		●		●		
Circle weave	111	Craft	4		●		●		●
Scrimshaw pendant	112	Craft	5		●		●		

Winter 113

December

Title	Page	Medium	Age	Prep 1	Prep 2	Prep 3	Help	Caution	Author
Cinnamon drawing	114	Drawing	3	●					
Fabric transfer	115	Drawing	3		●		●	●	●
Stained glass melt	116	Drawing	4		●		●	●	
Peeled glue	117	Drawing	4	●			●		
Paper drop dye	118	Painting	3		●				●
Shiny painting	119	Painting	3		●				
Insole stamps	120	Painting	4		●		●		
Stained glass painting	121	Painting	4	●					
Snow paint	122	Painting	4		●		●		
Window painting	123	Painting	5				●	●	
Sugar mint modelling	124	Dough	3		●		●		
Bread sculpture	125	Dough	4			●	●	●	●
Marzipan fantasy fruits	126	Dough	5				●	●	
Royal icing art	127	Sculpture	4				●	●	●
Sweet insects	128	Sculpture	5				●	●	
String ornaments	129	Craft	3	●			●		
Tile marking	130	Craft	3	●					

Spring 175

Introduction

It's the process, not the product

Young children "do" art for the experience, the exploration, the experimentation. In the "process" they discover mystery, creativity, joy, frustration. The resulting masterpiece, whether it be a sticky glob or meritorious gallery piece, is only a result to the young child, not the reason for doing art in the first place. Art allows children to explore and discover their world. Sometimes it is merely feeling slippery paint on the fingers, at other times it is the mystery of colours blending or the surprise of seeing a realistic picture evolve when blobs were randomly placed. Art can be a way to "get the wiggles out" or to smash a ball of clay instead of another child.

Sometimes adults unknowingly communicate to a child that the result is the most important aspect of art. Encourage discovery and process by talking with a child about his or her artwork:

- *Tell me about your painting.*
- *What part did you like best?*
- *You've used many colours.*
- *Did you enjoy making this?*
- *How did the paint feel?*
- *The yellow looks so bright next to the purple!*
- *How did you make such a big design?*
- *I see the painting is brown. What colours did you use?*

Providing interesting materials and watching what a child can do on his or her own is better than saying, "Paint a green fish in blue water." It can be far more exciting to paint on a piece of frozen paper or to paint with a feather instead of a brush, with no idea of what will happen, than to follow an adult's idea of what to paint.

Process art is a wonder to behold. Watch the children discover their capabilities and the joy of creativity.

Using *Preschool Art*

Preschool Art is filled with over 200 process art experiences for young children. The first chapter in the book is called The Basics. These projects are the basic art ideas every preschool child will want to experience. All the other projects in this book build on these basic art ideas. They can be done at any time during the year, experienced more than once (in fact many, many times) and they will always be of value to the developing young child.

The remaining four chapters are arranged by seasons and divided by months. For each month, you will find approximately 20 art ideas using four art categories: drawing, painting, sculpting with dough and clay, and crafts/constructing. The first three categories are the most process-oriented and open-ended art ideas. The constructing ideas are somewhat more craft than art, but still open-ended. Drawing indicates art ideas that involve pencils, crayons, pens and other drawing techniques such as drawing with glue, a finger in the sand or other unusual types of drawing. Painting could be painting with brushes or some other tool, using paint, food colouring or dye, or printing with a variety of materials. The sculpting projects involve using materials to make three-dimensional art ideas using a wealth and variety of art materials commonly found in the home or classroom. The construction projects tend to lean more towards crafts, but involve creative thinking in making puppets, wreathes, jewellery and other things.

There is one idea per page, complete with a materials list followed by steps in the art process with illustrations for each project. The upper page corner has icons that help the reader or artist quickly access the art idea with information on age, planning and preparation, safety and assistance needed. A side bar on the page tells the reader what type of art technique is featured in the project, such as painting, sculpture or drawing. At the bottom of each page is the name of the month to which the project has been assigned.

Using the seasonal chapters it is possible to follow along through the book page by page, day by day, and have plenty of process art experiences to last the entire year. However, it should be mentioned that choosing any project in the book at any time is also an exciting way to provide art for children.

Another way to select projects is by using the indexes. For instance, if you know you have ready-mixed paint and glue, look up ready-mixed paint or glue in the Materials Index.

Find those projects that use those materials and begin to select one that suits you and the young artist. Another good use for the Materials Index is to help you select and save materials for your art centre. Look through the index and note materials you have on hand as well as those you might start saving ahead of time.

Preschool Art is organized in a way to make process art experiences accessible, easy and developmentally appropriate. Provide the materials, stand back and enjoy the process of creative art!

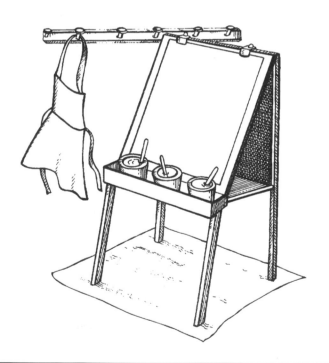

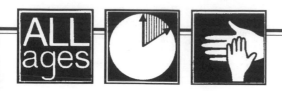

Chalk drawing

Materials
- chalk or pastels (many colours)
- paper
- hairspray, optional

Art process
1. Draw with coloured chalk on paper.
2. When the drawing is complete, an **adult** sprays it outside with hairspray to "set" the chalk and help prevent smudging. However, the chalk will still smudge a bit.

D R A W I N G

BASICS

HINT *Chalk smudges, but chalk is beautiful. Allow experimentation with the unique qualities of chalk and don't be too concerned with its inherent messiness. Children need to learn the qualities of chalk, and smudging is one of them.*

Wet chalk drawing

Materials
- sugar solution (70 g sugar to 230 ml water)
- container for sugar-water
- chalk
- paper
- hairspray, optional

Art process
1. Soak poster chalk overnight in sugar solution.
2. Draw with the wet chalk on paper.
3. The sugar-water helps brighten the chalk colours and keeps the drawing from smearing too much.
4. Dry the completed art project.
5. An **adult** can spray the completed drawing with hairspray (outside) if a completely non-smear drawing is desired.

Variation
- Dip the end of the chalk into the sugar-water in the small container and draw on paper with dampened chalk.

Container for sugar-water

70 g sugar

RUMP HAIR SPRAY

230 ml water

Paper

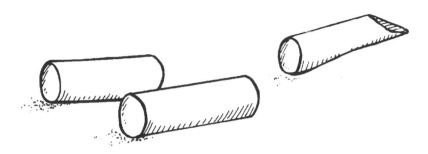

HINT Keep in mind that chalk has unique qualities: it breaks easily; it smudges; it does not act like crayon; it can be brushed with a cotton wool ball, cotton swab or tissue; its colours can be blended, used brightly or lightly; it can be crushed and used as a powder; powdered chalk can be mixed to make new chalk colours; it is messy and beautiful.

DRAWING

BASICS

Dry chalk, wet paper

D
R
A
W
I
N
G

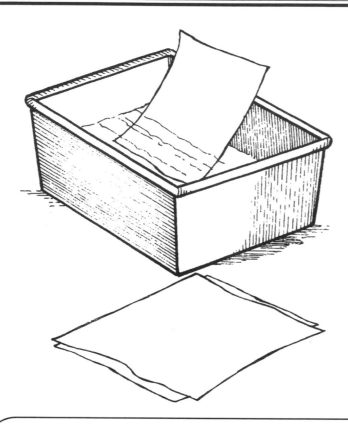

Materials
- container with about 10 cm of water in it
- chalk or pastels
- assorted papers

Art process
1. Dip the paper into the water, thoroughly coating it with water. Place it on a dry table.
2. Draw with dry chalk or pastels on the wet paper.
3. Experiment with different textures and types of paper.
4. Lift the completed project from the table and dry on newspaper.
5. Dry for one or two days.

Variations
- Experiment with a paintbrush dipped in clear water on dry paper. Paint a design with the water and then draw with chalk or pastels on the watery design.
- Try rubbing the chalk drawing with a cotton wool ball or tissue to smudge, blend or smear.

Chalk behaves somewhat like paint on wet paper: it can be blended or smeared.

Sometimes it helps to break large pieces of chalk in half or into smaller pieces for younger artists.

PASTELS

Chalk and liquid starch

Materials
- small containers filled with liquid starch
- small paintbrushes
- chalk or pastels

Art process
1. Brush the starch over the paper.
2. Draw on the paper with chalk or pastels.
3. The liquid starch brightens the chalk colours and reduces the powdery smudging of the chalk drawing. The drawing will still smudge.
4. Dry the completed art project.

Variation
- Dip the end of the chalk into the starch in the small container and draw on paper with dampened chalk.

BASICS

HINT Sometimes it helps to break big pieces of chalk in half or into smaller pieces for young children.

Liquid starch can be saved and re-used for other projects requiring liquid starch.

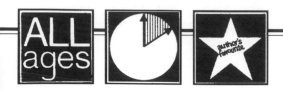

D R A W I N G

Scribbler

Materials
- crayons
- variety of papers

Art process
1. Use big circular motions or free movement to create the outline of the artwork.
2. Colour in the "holes" of the design, if desired.

Variations
- Use big paper for really big arm movements.
- Colour to the rhythm of music.

BASICS

HINT

Expect lots of noise and very energetic arms because this project is really fun for young artists.

Big arm movements also mean torn paper if a crayon catches the edge of the paper. Tape the paper to the table or easel.

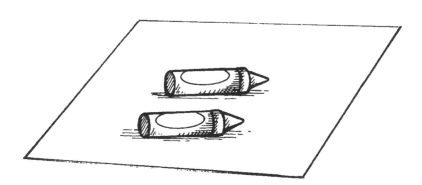

Free drawing

Materials
- crayons
- variety of papers with different textures, colours and sizes
- tables, easels or floor

Art process
1. Use the crayon to draw on the paper.
2. Experiment with different textures, colours and sizes of papers.
3. Draw on paper placed on the flat surface of a table or floor, or use the upright surface of an easel.

Variations
- If the artist expresses some description about the drawing, the words can be written on the front or back of the drawing. You may want to write on a strip of paper that the artist can attach to the drawing themselves. Most art professionals feel it is best not to write directly on the artwork unless the artist specifically wishes it to be placed there.
- Provide other drawing tools such as charcoal, pencils, coloured pencils, fine or wide point felt pens, pastels, chalk, fabric pens or any drawing tools available.

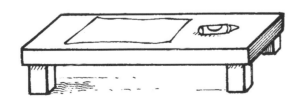

HINT *Use free drawing often with artists.*

The possibilities of free drawing are endless and varied.

BASICS

D R A W I N G

Crayon rubbing

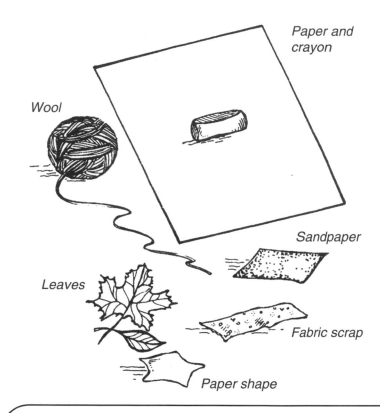

Paper and crayon

Wool

Sandpaper

Leaves

Fabric scrap

Paper shape

Materials
- large, peeled crayons
- lining paper or sugar paper
- objects with textures for rubbings—pieces of wool, pieces of sandpaper, shapes cut or torn from heavy paper, leaves, scraps of fabric glued to cards, other flat or textured items

Art process
1. Place chosen objects under the heavy paper.
2. Tape the corners of the paper to the work surface to prevent the paper from shifting.
3. Holding the paper down with one hand, gently rub the flat side of the crayon over the covered objects.
4. An imprint of the covered object will appear on the paper.

BASICS

HINT *Younger children will achieve varying degrees of quality with rubbings. Age and experience will affect the final outcome. Expect vigorous movements and torn or wiggling paper if the project is not taped to the work surface.*

More rub-a-rub

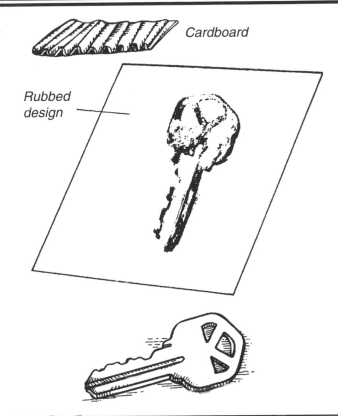

Cardboard

Rubbed design

Materials
- large sheets of paper
- large, peeled crayons
- surfaces such as wood grain, tree bark, concrete, walls, bricks, tiles, leather and signs with raised or recessed letters
- textures such as bumpy greetings cards, coins, licence plates, corrugated cardboard, lace doilies, a comb, a piece of screen or a grill

Art process
1. Place a large sheet of paper over any of the surfaces or textures listed above.
2. Rub the covered area with a large, peeled crayon held on its side.
3. Move on to another texture or surface, collecting the designs from as many objects as desired.

Variation
- Use the textures or rubbed designs to "colour in" a picture. For example, rub over buttons for eyes, flock wallpaper for clothing, tree bark for hair and so on.

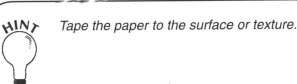

HINT *Tape the paper to the surface or texture.*

BASICS

D R A W I N G

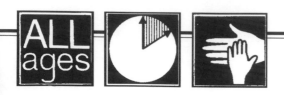

Body trace

Materials
- large sheets of lining paper
- crayon or felt pen
- paints and brushes, optional
- fabric scraps and glue, optional
- large floor space
- scissors

Art process
1. The artist must lie down on a large sheet of lining paper stretched out on the floor. Arms and legs should be spread out a little so they can be easily traced.
2. A second person takes a pen or crayon and traces the entire body of the artist including fingers, hair and other details.
3. When the tracing is complete, the artist can jump up and decide how to enhance the shape with paints, crayons, felt pens or fabric scraps and glue.
4. The object is to add all the features of the real person who was traced.
5. When the decorating and designing is complete, cut out the shape and tape it to the wall with feet touching the ground and the head at child height.

Variations
- A silhouette can be made using the same method. Use black paper and white chalk to complete this variation of the project.
- The shape can be decorated to look different from the person who was traced, such as a being from outer space, a mother, a baker or some other character.

HINT *Sometimes young artists are surprised and even disappointed with the tracing done by another person. You may wish to have teenagers, parents or other grown-up volunteers do the tracing rather than other young artists.*

BASICS

Mark making

Materials
- paper or other material to mark on
- tools to make marks—pencils, chalk, crayons, markers or pastels
- design tools such as a ruler, protractor, stencils, templates, lids, tops or objects to trace

Art process
1. Select a drawing tool and start making marks on a selected material such as paper.
2. Explore and experiment with different marking and design tools. For instance, trace the lids of jars and overlap the circle shapes or make ruler lines of measured lengths with chalk. The possibilities are unlimited. The idea is to provide the markers and design tools and let the artists explore their imagination.

Variation
- Make marks with paint. Dip the design tools in the paint and then place them on the paper to make a design. Make marks in the sand or earth. Make footprints or hand prints. The possibilities are endless.

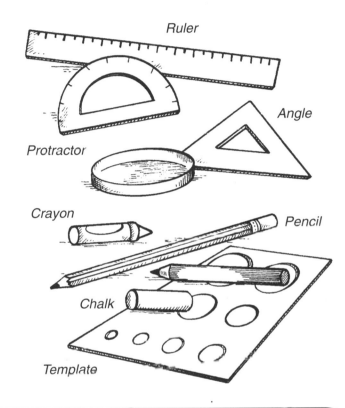

Ruler

Angle

Protractor

Crayon

Pencil

Chalk

Template

DRAWING

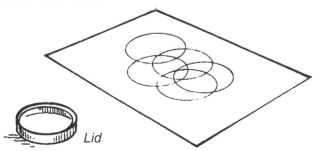

Lid

HINT *The key to developing a creative imagination is to stand back and let the artists make their own discoveries. Let the artists explore and create, sharing their delight with different results and processes.*

BASICS

Sand and glue drawing

BASICS

HINT Clean sand can be purchased from hardware or toy shops.

If blobs of glue-sand fall into the tub from the paper, let them dry and remove when hardened.

Materials
- sand in large, wide tub (a sand table works well)
- PVA glue in bottles
- PVA glue in cup with a paintbrush or cotton bud
- paper, posterpaper or board

Art process
1. Place a sheet of paper, posterpaper or board in the tub on the surface of the sand.
2. Draw a design on the paper with the glue from a bottle or with a paintbrush dipped in the cup of glue.
3. When the design is complete, scoop handfuls of sand from the tub and cover the entire paper with sand.
4. Pick up the paper from the corner and let the excess sand fall back into the tub.
5. Set sand drawing aside to dry.

Variations
- Fill a yoghurt pot half-full of sand, add some powdered paint and stir the sand and paint together to make coloured sand. Make several colours in different cups. Use the coloured sand for drawings by sprinkling pinches and bits of sand in specific places on the design.
- Make sand drawings on the playground or the pavement. Do not use any glue. Simply squeeze dry sand from a squeezy ketchup bottle making lines, dots and other designs directly on the pavement. Sweep away the sand when complete.

Ironed greaseproof paper

Materials
- old pieces of crayons, peeled
- old cheese grater
- greaseproof paper cut into 20 cm x 25 cm pieces
- newspaper
- old iron, set on warm
- scissors
- wool, optional

Art process
1. Work on a thick pad of newspaper.
2. Place a sheet of greaseproof paper on the newspaper.
3. Grate crayons on to the sheet of greaseproof paper.
4. Cover the crayon shavings and greaseproof paper with a second sheet of greaseproof paper.
5. Cover this with another sheet of newspaper.
6. **Adult** irons over the newspaper to melt the crayon shavings beneath and "glue" greaseproof paper pieces together.
7. Remove the top newspaper. Trim the excess edges of the greaseproof paper with scissors. Glue a piece of wool to the project if the artist wishes to hang the design in a window.

Variations
- Greaseproof paper can be used in a variety of sizes or shapes. You may choose to frame the finished project with coloured paper.
- Sometimes pressing straight down with the iron and then lifting it straight up (instead of rubbing it back and forth) creates different designs in the melted crayon.

Wool

HINT

With careful supervision the artist can do the ironing. Most children can be very careful.

Tape the iron cord in place so artists in the room don't trip over it.

This project should be supervised by an adult at all times.

BASICS

   caution author's favourite ALL ages

Warm crayon

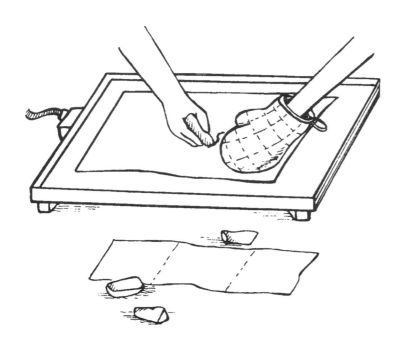

HINT

Artists must be told to keep hands and arms off the warming tray.

Tape the electric cord to the table with masking tape.

This project should be supervised by an adult at all times.

Materials
- electric food-warming tray (look at jumble/car boot sales and in charity shops)
- paper
- old crayons, peeled
- oven glove or similar thick glove
- masking tape, optional
- paper towels

Art process
1. Turn on the warming tray to a very warm setting, but not dangerously hot.
2. Place a piece of paper on the warmed tray. **Adult** tapes the paper to the tray to hold it in place.
3. Wear a thick glove or oven glove on the non-drawing hand. Use this hand to hold the paper still.
4. With the free drawing hand, move a crayon slowly over the heated paper and make a melted design.
5. Wipe the warming tray with a paper towel after each use and the warm, melted crayon wax spills will disappear quickly, leaving a clean tray for the next artist.

Variation
- Cover the tray with heavy-duty aluminium foil. Draw directly on the warm foil. Press a paper towel or piece of paper on to the melted design, peel the paper off and observe the design transferred to the paper. Remember to wipe the tray clean with a paper towel to remove the excess crayon design.

Edible powder paint

Edible dusting powder is a harmless food colouring. Although fairly expensive, it it worth buying as it makes the best paint I have ever used.

Materials
- 1/8 teaspoon edible dusting powder
- 1 tablespoon water
- liquid starch
- mixing jug
- measuring spoons
- stirring spoon

Art process
1. Dissolve the edible dusting powder in the water.
2. Add liquid starch to reach desired colour intensity.
3. Stir the mixture.
4. Paint as with any paint.

Variations
- Edible dusting powder mixed with wallpaper paste or hobby and craft paste makes a brilliant and translucent paint.
- Food colouring is a substitute for edible dusting powder.
- To make a more intense colour, use half a teaspoon of powder.

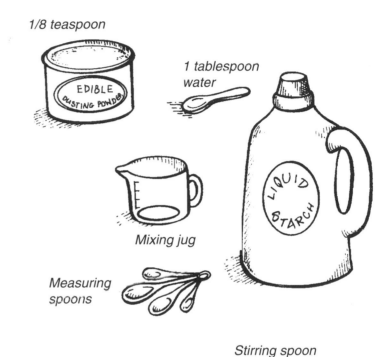

1/8 teaspoon

1 tablespoon water

Mixing jug

Measuring spoons

Stirring spoon

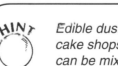

HINT

Edible dusting powder is available from specialist cake shops in a wide variety of colours. The powders can be mixed to make new colours.

Paint from edible dusting powder is somewhat transparent.

BASICS

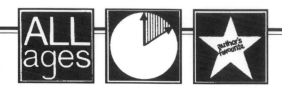

Free paint

Brushes

Cloth

Paper

BASICS

HINT

Free painting is simply painting on paper with no particular expectations from anyone. There is no end to the possibilities of what will emerge from free painting.

Materials
- ready-mixed paints with brushes
- cup of water for rinsing
- cloth for drying
- any paper
- work surface such as floor, table, easel, wall or board for the lap

Art process
1. Choose a paper and a work surface.
2. Choose a colour of paint.
3. Begin painting on the paper, rinsing the brush when changing colours.
4. Paint until the design is complete. The work can be a design, a pattern or a more realistic rendering. Whatever the artist paints is acceptable.
5. Dry the work on the work surface or remove to a drying area.

Variations
- Experiment with different textures of paper, different mixtures of thick and thin ready-mixed paints and different amounts of water used for the watercolour paints.
- Experiment with mixing colours.
- Sometimes it is interesting to alter the paper used for painting. For example, cut the paper in a variety of shapes or cut out shapes from a piece of paper to be painted. Newspaper or wrapping paper can also be used as a surface for painting designs.

Watercolour paint

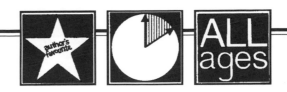

Materials
- watercolour paint box and paintbrush
- cup of water for rinsing
- paper
- cloth for drying
- newspaper-covered work surface

Art process
1. Dip a paintbrush in the clear water and then into one of the watercolour paint colours.
2. Paint on the paper.
3. Rinse the brush in the clear water and continue painting with the watercolour paints.
4. Change the rinse water when it gets murky.
5. Paint until the artwork is complete.
6. Dry on the work surface or move to a drying area by lifting the entire sheet of newspaper and carrying the painting on the newspaper.

Variations
- Experiment with mixing colours in the lid of the paint box or on the paper.
- Paint on wet paper.
- Outline dry designs with permanent felt pen.
- Sprinkle the paint with salt.

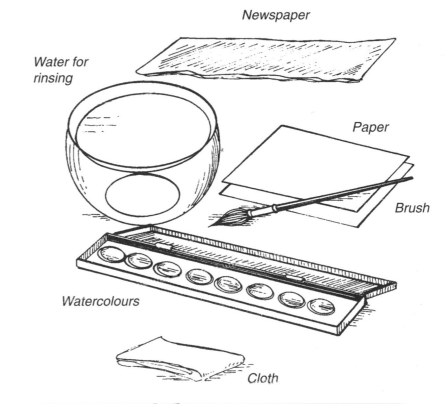

Newspaper

Water for rinsing

Paper

Brush

Watercolours

Cloth

HINT

Young artists often hold up their paintings for adults to admire. Watercolour paintings are usually dripping wet which can be a bit messy. Remind artists to hold their wet creations "flat" or call the adult to their work spot for viewing the creation.

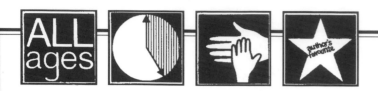

Fingerpainting

PAINTING

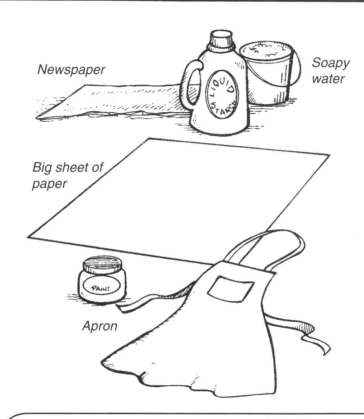

Newspaper

Soapy water

Big sheet of paper

Apron

BASICS

HINT

Glossy or shiny papers work best.

This is a messy project. Even artists who cover their clothing still seem to get paint on their clothes.

Materials

- powdered or ready-mixed paint
- liquid starch
- big sheet of paper
- newspaper
- cover artist in apron or big shirt
- soapy water in bucket and towel

Art process

1. Open a full sheet of newspaper and place on the floor or table.
2. Place a large piece of paper on the newspaper.
3. Pour a puddle of liquid starch about the size of a piece of bread in the middle of the paper.
4. Place a squeeze of ready-mixed paint or a rounded spoonful of powdered paint in the middle of the starch puddle.
5. Begin to smear and mix the paint and starch by hand.
6. When paint is spread across the paper, begin to fingerpaint by drawing fingers and hands through the paint. Elbows and arms make interesting designs too.
7. If paint dries out, add a bit more starch to the paper.
8. When painting is complete, lift entire sheet of newspaper with painting on it and carry to a drying area.
9. When dry, peel the finished project carefully from the newspaper. You may wish to place the artwork on a clean sheet of newspaper before drying to prevent painting from sticking to the newspaper.

Easel painting

Materials
- paint easel with clips for paper
- covered easel board
- large sheets of newsprint or lining paper
- paints in cups
- large paintbrush for each cup
- covered floor under easel
- paint apron or big shirt for artist

Art process
1. Clip a small stack of paper to the easel. (The top piece can be slipped out when painting is complete; the next piece of paper will be ready for the artist.)
2. Fill the cups with paints mixed to a medium consistency that will avoid runny drips. Use cups with snap-on lids containing a hole for the brush. Yoghurt pots also work well, as do small milk cartons. Both of these versions can be thrown away after using for a period of time.
3. Dip brushes into paint and paint on the paper (see hint).
4. When painting is complete, remove the painting from the easel and clip to a drying rack until dry. A fish net on the wall with clothes pegs provides a good drying area.

Variation
- Place other art media at the easel such as chalk, watercolours, felt pens or unusual paint recipes such as vegetable dye paint (see page 27).

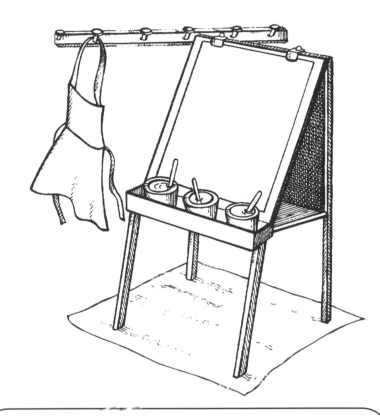

PAINTING

HINT *Young artists do not have the adult concept of keeping brushes in only one colour of paint or keeping cups of paint clean. Young artists are involved in painting and mixing colours. As much as adults would like the cups of paint to stay clean and unmixed with other colours, it may not happen.*

BASICS

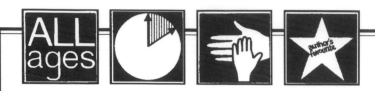

Paint dough

Water

Bowls

Squeezy bottles

Materials
- flour
- water
- salt
- ready-mixed paint
- measuring jug
- bowls, mixing spoons
- posterpaper or board
- plastic squeezy bottles

Art process
1. Mix equal parts of flour and salt to form a paste consistency.
2. Add paint to create the desired colour. Make several different colours.
3. Pour paint mixture into plastic squeezy bottle.
4. Squeeze paint on to the posterpaper or board to make designs.
5. Dry the completed project. The salt gives the designs a glistening crystal quality when dry.

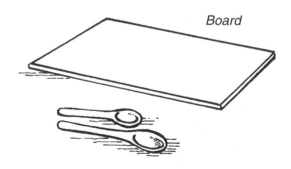

Board

BASICS

HINT

Different colours of paint mixtures will not mix together when colours bump into each other. They maintain their own separate design and space, which is different from regular paints.

Paint mixture can dry and harden in squeezy bottles so rinse bottles clean when project is complete.

P A I N T I N G

Runnies

Materials

- several colours of ready-mixed paint
- cups
- spoons for each colour
- paper
- masking tape, optional
- baking tray

Art process

1. Place a piece of paper on a baking tray. Tape the corners to hold the paper in place.
2. Mix several colours of ready-mixed paint in cups to a thin consistency and place a spoon in each cup of paint.
3. Spoon one colour of paint on the paper. Next, tip the baking tray to make the colour run across the paper making tracks.
4. Now add another colour. Tip the baking tray again. The colours will run into each other and mix.
5. Add as many colours and tip as many times as desired.
6. When finished, remove the paper from the baking tray and place in a drying area. You may also choose to dry the painting on the baking tray and remove later.

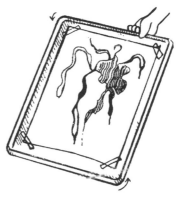

Variation

- Place a puddle of paint on the paper and blow the paint in different directions using a drinking straw. Remind the artist to blow out only so no paint will be accidently swallowed!

HINT — *Thick paint runs too but may need a little coaxing with a paintbrush or toothpick to get it started.*

The baking tray helps control spills and drips. It works best if it has sides.

BASICS

PAINTING

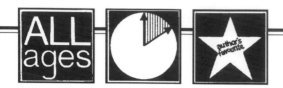

P
A
I
N
T
I
N
G

Paint blots

Materials
- ready-mixed paints in cups
- spoon or paintbrush for each colour
- paper, pre-folded down the middle
- covered work surface
- scissors, optional

Art process
1. Place the pre-folded piece of paper on the covered work surface and open it out flat.
2. Drop blobs of paint on the fold or on one side of the paper.
3. Fold over the other side of the paper and rub or press the paper very gently. Pressing outwards from the fold spreads the paint out on to the paper.
4. Unfold the paper to see what the "blot" looks like.
5. Make more blots on new paper. Think about what shapes might occur and what colours might mix together.
6. Dry the completed project. Cut out the design if desired.

Variations
- Make huge blots on huge paper.
- Blots can be cut out and made into butterflies, flowers, insects or other imaginary things.
- For the more advanced artistic thinker, attempt to make shapes such as a heart, snowflake, face or other form.

BASICS

HINT *Pressing gently seems to be an important factor in making blots that appeal to artists. To test the technique, make a blot by pressing really hard. Next make another one by pressing gently. Decide which technique suits the artist.*

Monoprint

Materials
- washable table
- powdered paint
- liquid starch
- spoon
- paintbrush
- paper
- newspaper-covered drying area

Art process
1. Pour a puddle of liquid starch in the artist's work space.
2. Add a spoonful of powdered paint to the puddle.
3. Mix the starch and paint with hands or a paintbrush, spreading it out on the table to a size that will fit the piece of paper.
4. Draw a design in the paint using the fingers.
5. When the design is complete, gently place the sheet of paper over the design and pat without pressing too hard.
6. Lift the paper from the design by the corner, peeling it away from the paint.
7. A monoprint of the design will be on the paper. Place the paper on some newspaper to dry.
8. Additional prints may be made from the same design or a new design can be made and printed.

Variations
- Add more than one colour of paint to the puddle of starch and experiment with combinations of colours and mixing colours.
- Instead of painting on the table top, paint on a sheet of plastic or on a baking tray.

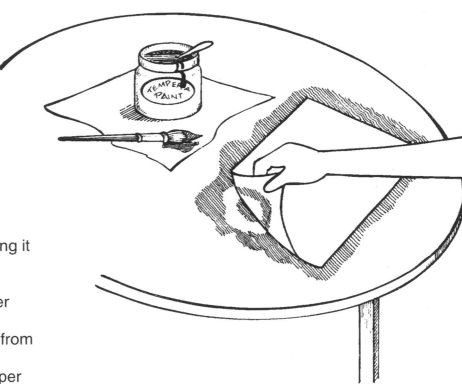

HINT

If the paint on the table dries out, add more starch to make it smooth and ready again.

Curled, dry paintings can be ironed to flatten.

BASICS

PAINTING

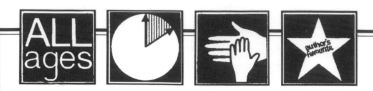

Dip and dye papers

Materials
- one of the following papers—coffee filters, paper towels, napkins, ink blotter or white tissue paper
- covered table
- sheets of newsprint
- cups of food colouring or paper dye
- eyedroppers
- drying area

Art process
1. Cover a table with thick layers of newspaper.
2. Place sheets of newsprint around the table like placemats where each artist will work.
3. There are several techniques in "dip and dye". The easiest one is to first place a paper towel on the newsprint and then squeeze drops of food colouring or paper dye on to the paper towel. Another technique is to fold the paper towel and then dip the corners of the towel into the cups of dye. Unfold carefully and place the towel on the sheet of newsprint. A coffee filter is perhaps the best paper to fold and dip in the cups of dye.
4. Experiment with dipping and dyeing any of the papers suggested.
5. Carry the wet dyed towel or paper on the sheet of newsprint to a drying area and dry for an hour or so. If dyeing a thin paper such as white tissue, unfold the wet dyed paper as far as possible without tearing and dry overnight. Finish unfolding the dry paper the next day. When completely dry, iron the paper with adult help if necessary.

BASICS

HINT

Paper dyes are available from art shops in jars of highly concentrated powdered dyes. Although fairly expensive, the dyes will last for years and the colours are incredibly bright and vibrant. In the long run, the powdered dyes are cheaper and better than food colouring.

Paint and print

Materials

- things to use for making prints—kitchen utensils, gadgets, toys, sponges, fingertips or inflated balloons
- ready-mixed paints
- bowl or tray
- paper towels
- paintbrush
- paper
- covered work surface

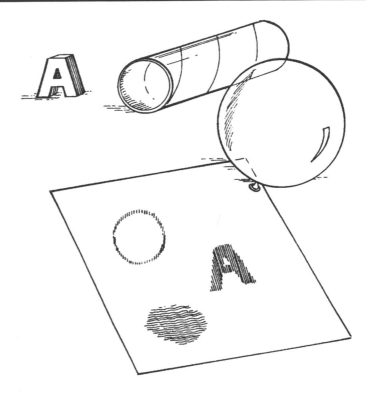

Art process

1. Place a pad of wet paper towels in the bowl or tray.
2. Spread ready-mixed paint on the paper towels for a print pad.
3. Press an object into the paint and then press it on to the paper. Press the object on the paper several times before replacing it in the paint. Random designs or patterns are two of the design possibilities.
4. Dry the design on the work surface or move the wet design to a drying area.

Variations

- Experiment printing with ink, food colouring, watercolour paints, thick and thin paint or paper, or fabric dye.
- Make wrapping paper, a wall hanging, greetings cards, a framed poster or simply enjoy the artwork and eventually discard.
- Wrap string around a block of wood or toilet paper tube for a string print.
- Cut cardboard shapes and glue to a block of wood for a relief print.

HINT *Encourage young artists to press the object gently into the paint and then on to the paper because it makes a better print. Some young minds think that the harder and louder you whack the object into the paint and then on to the paper, the more impressive the print will be.*

P A I N T I N G

BASICS

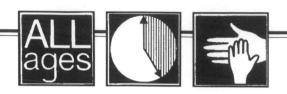

Handy prints (footie, too)

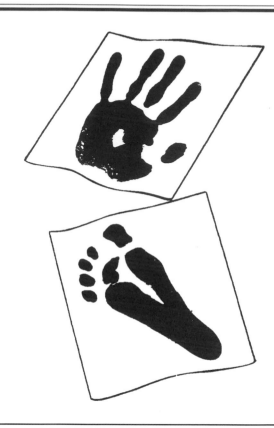

Materials
- hands and feet
- thick ready-mixed paints and paintbrush
- shallow tray
- paper
- covered work surface
- bucket of soapy water and towels

Art process
1. Pour several colours of thick ready-mixed paints into separate trays. Three different colours are appropriate.
2. Paint the artist's hand with a brush or press the hand into the paint.
3. The artist presses the painted hand on to the paper. Press again on the paper without repainting, if desired.
4. Re-paint the hand in a new colour or the same colour. Continue printing on the paper. Overlap colours to make new colours.
5. Wash and dry hands before carrying the print to a drying area.
6. Make foot prints too! Follow the same procedures using the artist's foot instead of hand. Walk on a long pieces of paper or make single prints on small pieces of paper.

Variations
- Make a single hand print on a paper plate.
- Use both hands, feet, elbows or the nose to make prints. Have fun! This is a good project to do outside.

BASICS

HINT *A hand-washing bucket or a large, shallow tub usually works better than a sink. A bucket is easy to clean and easy for the kids to use. Make sure you change the water in the bucket often if hands and feet are printing. The paint usually stains the skin but wears away in a day or two.*

Stone painting

Materials

- flat stones, any size
- ready-mixed paints in cups
- medium point paintbrushes
- newspaper-covered work area
- clear acrylic craft paint, optional

Art process

1. Collect flat stones at the beach, along the river or purchase from a garden centre.
2. This project may be completed outdoors or inside.
3. Place stones on a work surface covered with newspaper.
4. Dip a medium point brush into the paint and paint a design on the stone.
5. If painting the underside of the stone too, let the top dry before turning it over. When dry, turn the stone over and paint the underside of the stone.
6. **Adult** covers the design with a clear acrylic craft paint to protect the design if desired.

Variations

- When the basic design is dry on the stone, use a fine point brush to add details.
- Use felt pens for the design or to add details to a dry, painted stone.
- Use the finished products for paperweights, bookends or table decorations.
- Stack and glue stones together to make painted stone sculptures.

HINT *Older children can use acrylic paints which won't wash or smudge off the stone when dry.*

BASICS

Craft clay

Flour

Water

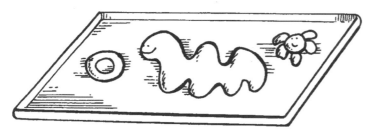

Materials
- 800 g flour
- 200 g salt
- bowl
- 350 ml warm water
- wooden spoon
- baking tray
- chopping board
- cling film
- foil or greaseproof paper
- oven

Art process
1. Combine the flour and salt in a bowl.
2. Make a well in the centre of the dry ingredients and pour in one cup warm water. Mix the dough with your hands.
3. Add more water and continue mixing. The dough should not be crumbly or sticky, but should form a ball.
4. Knead the dough on a floured board until smooth (about five minutes).
5. Work with a small portion of dough at a time on a piece of foil or greaseproof paper. Keep the rest of the dough wrapped in cling film and in the fridge. (If it dries out, add a few drops of water and knead.) All dough parts should be joined together with water, using a brush or fingers.
6. When a sculpture or object is complete, **adult** places it on a foil-covered baking sheet and bakes at 325ºF (170ºC) for one hour or until hard. Dough should not "give" when tapped with a knife.

Variation
- Some ideas for things to make include napkin rings; jewellery; beads; pretend rolls or bread; pretend fruits; vegetables and play foods; picture frames; insects; animals; or festive decorations.

BASICS

HINT

Work directly on a baking sheet to prevent tearing or breaking the objects when moving them.

Breaks and cracks in baked pieces can be repaired with PVA glue forced into the crack, or fresh dough can be pressed between broken pieces, re-baked and then covered with paint.

Yeast dough

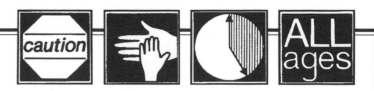

Materials

- 1 tablespoon yeast
- 350 ml warm water
- 1 teaspoon salt
- 1 tablespoon sugar
- 800 g flour
- measuring jug and spoons
- large bowl and mixing spoon
- greased baking tray
- pastry brush
- 1 egg, beaten
- salt, optional
- oven

Art process

1. With adult help, measure 350 ml warm water into the large bowl. Sprinkle yeast into water and stir until soft.
2. Add the salt, sugar and flour. Mix until dough forms a ball.
3. Knead on floured surface until smooth and elastic.
4. Roll and twist dough into shapes such as letters, animals and unique shapes.
5. Place the dough sculptures on a greased baking tray. Cover and let rise in a warm place until double in size.
6. Brush each sculpture with beaten egg. Sprinkle with salt (optional).
7. **Adult** bakes for 12 to 15 minutes at 350ºF (180ºC) until sculptures are firm and golden brown.
8. Cool slightly. Eat and enjoy! Yum!

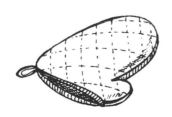 

HINT *Use this delicious dough to make healthy, seasonal treats such as pumpkin faces in the autumn, snowflakes in the winter, bunnies in the spring and great big suns in the summer.*

BASICS

CLAY

Playful clay

Materials
- measuring jugs
- saucepan
- 200 g bicarbonate of soda
- 100 g cornflour
- 150 ml warm water
- food colouring or ready-mixed paints
- cooker
- chopping board
- newspaper
- clear nail polish, optional

Art process
1. Mix bicarbonate of soda and cornflour in a saucepan.
2. Add water and stir until smooth.
3. **Adult** places the pan over medium heat. Boil and stir until the consistency of mashed potatoes. Pour the mixture on to the chopping board to cool.
4. Knead the dough when cool.
5. For colour, knead food colouring into clay until blended. Objects may also be painted when completely dry.
6. Explore and create with the playful clay.
7. When objects are complete, harden or dry on newspaper for several hours.
8. For a shine, **adult** paints the dry objects with clear nail polish.

Variation
- Crush coloured chalk and knead into the dough for a speckled colouring.

BASICS

HINT

This recipe makes one and a half cups of dough. It can be doubled easily.

The dough stores in an airtight container for several weeks but will dry out if exposed to the air.

This material hardens quickly.

Cooked playdough

Materials

- measuring cups and spoons
- 200 g flour
- 200 g salt
- 230 ml water
- 1 tablespoon cream of tartar
- food colouring
- saucepan
- cooker
- spoon
- chopping board
- cooking utensils for sculpting and play
- plastic container with lid for storage

Art process

1. With an adult, mix the flour, water, salt and cream of tartar in a saucepan. (For coloured dough, add food colouring to the water and mix with the other ingredients.)
2. **Adult** places the pan over low heat and stirs until the dough forms a ball.
3. Remove the pan from the heat, pour the ball on a chopping board and knead until smooth and pliable.
4. Give the warm dough to the artist to begin sculpting, exploring, playing and creating. Provide any variety of utensils and tools for exploration such as a rolling pin or wooden dowel, cookie cutters, a fork, nuts and bolts or a garlic press.
5. The dough can be stored in a plastic container for a week or so.

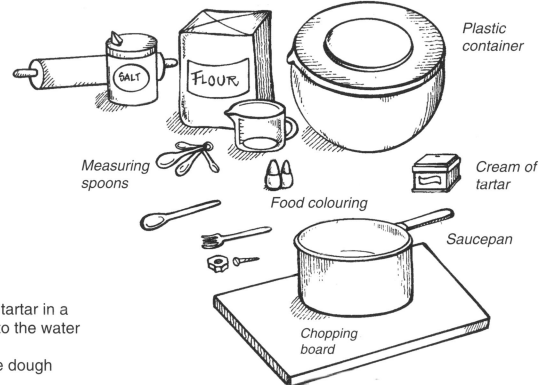

Plastic container

Measuring spoons

Cream of tartar

Food colouring

Saucepan

Chopping board

C L A Y

HINT

When playdough begins to crack and crumble, it's time for a fresh batch.

Double this recipe for twice as much fun.

BASICS

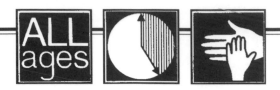

No-cook playdough

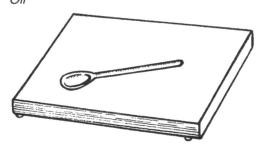

Oil

Water

Materials
- measuring jugs and spoons
- 230 ml cold water
- 200 g salt
- 2 teaspoons oil
- 600 g flour
- 2 tablespoons cornflour
- powdered paint or food colouring
- bowl and spoon
- chopping board

Art process
1. In a bowl mix the water, salt, oil and enough powdered paint to make a bright colour.
2. Gradually work flour and cornflour into the mixture until it reaches a bread dough consistency.
3. Pour the dough on to a chopping board and knead.
4. Use this dough to model as with any clay.

Variation
- Colour the dough with food colouring or paste colouring.

 HINT *This quick and easy clay does not dry well but is a pliable, bright and colourful modelling clay.*

Great goop

Materials

- one part cornflour
- one part water
- plastic tub or large baking pan
- measuring jugs
- spoon
- food colouring, optional

Art process

1. Mix the cornflour with water in a large measuring jug. With one cup of cornflour, use one cup of water. With four cups of cornflour, use four cups of water and so on.
2. Add food colouring if desired. It is not necessary.
3. Pour the mixture into a tub or large baking pan.
4. Begin to experience and enjoy this unique mixture's properties and surprises.

Variations

- Add more cornflour or more water and see what happens to the mixture.
- Make goop mixture in a water table or large tub for a group experience. Add utensils such as a spatula, rolling pin or whisk to manipulate the mixture.

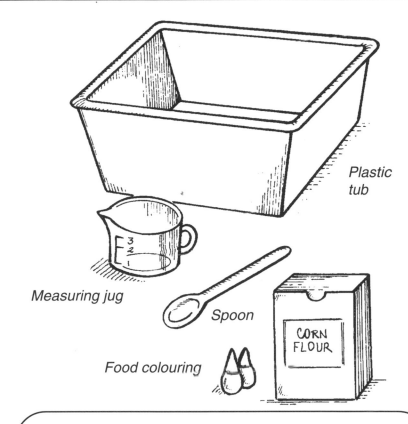

Plastic tub

Measuring jug

Spoon

Food colouring

CORN FLOUR

BASICS

HINT

Do not pour the goop mixture down the sink when exploring is complete. Scoop it into a paper or plastic bag and discard in the rubbish bin.

This is a very messy but wonderful project! Have a hand-washing bucket nearby for easy clean-up.

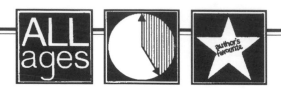

Peanut butter dough

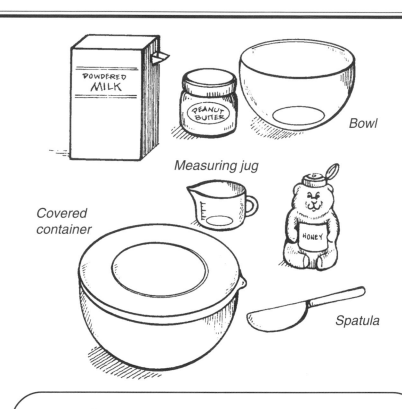

Powdered Milk

Peanut Butter

Bowl

Measuring jug

Covered container

Honey

Spatula

Materials
- measuring jug and spoons
- 1 part peanut butter
- 1 part skimmed dry milk (powdered milk)
- 1 tablespoon honey, optional
- bowl
- spatula
- kneading surface
- covered container

Art process
1. Wash and dry hands before beginning this edible dough.
2. Mix equal parts of peanut butter and dry milk together in a bowl by hand.
3. Add honey if desired.
4. Knead and mix the dough until it has a stiff, dough-like consistency.
5. Model and experiment with the peanut butter dough like any playdough.
6. Eat and enjoy your art creation!

Variation
- Add other ingredients such as raisins, shredded coconut, chocolate chips or bits of dry breakfast cereal into the dough or use to decorate the dough designs.

BASICS

HINT

Avoid this activity if someone in the group suffers from a nut allergy.

One cup of peanut butter and one cup of dry milk makes a nice ball of dough for one child.

This dough models fairly well but does not harden.

It keeps well in a covered container in the fridge.

Soap clay

Materials
- 400 g white detergent flakes
- 2 tablespoons water
- food colouring, optional
- bowl

Art process
1. Pour detergent into a bowl.
2. Add water or coloured water gradually while mixing and squeezing with hands until soap forms a ball.
3. Add more water if necessary.
4. Model and explore soap clay, squeezing and forming different shapes.
5. Clean-up is easy with warm water and a towel handy. Hands are already soapy!

Variations
- Make soap balls to use at home or school.
- Give soap balls or soap shapes as gifts.
- Mix natural materials into soap clay such as porridge oats or crushed dried flower petals.
- Add fragrance to the soap clay with spices such as cinnamon or with extracts such as almond or lemon.
- Try carving the soap clay with a spoon, toothpick or other tool.

Water

Bowl

WHITE DETERGENT FLAKES

HINT Once in a while someone will put a soapy finger in his or her mouth. The adult should calmly provide clear water and a cup at the sink. Keep rinsing out the mouth until the taste is gone. If someone gets soap in his or her eye, flood the eye with clear water until the stinging is gone.

BASICS

Collage

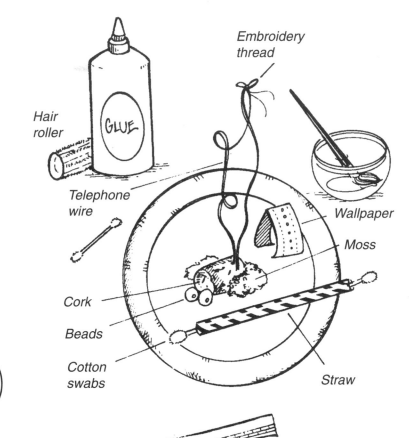

Hair roller

GLUE

Embroidery thread

Telephone wire

Wallpaper

Moss

Cork

Beads

Cotton swabs

Straw

Zip

Materials
- any collage items (see suggestions below)
- PVA glue in a squeezY bottle or PVA glue thinned with water in a cup with a paintbrush
- materials for a base such as paper, wood, cardboard, an old file folder, board, a paper plate, a styrofoam tray or box

Art process
1. Using glue, stick any collage items to a chosen base.
2. Any design and any amount or type of collage items make each collage unique.
3. Dry the project completely, sometimes overnight if the glue is very thick.

Variations
- A group can work on a collage together with everyone participating on a large base.
- Choose a theme for a collage such as shapes, colours, plants, happiness, good foods or textures.
- The following is a small list of collage suggestions: acorns, aluminum foil, bark, beads, bolts, bones, bottle caps, cellophane, confetti, cork, cotton, cotton buds, eggshells, embroidery thread, fabric, feathers, felt, flowers, glitter, hair grips, hair rollers, hooks, ice-cream sticks, jewellery, keys, lace, moss, newspapers, origami paper, paper dots, pebbles, pine cones, ribbons, sawdust, shells, stars, sticks, stones, string, telephone wire, tiles, toothpicks, vermiculite, wallpaper, wood scraps, wood shavings, wooden beads, wool, wrapping paper or zips.

C O L L A G E

BASICS

Tissue collage

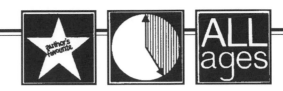

Materials
- art tissue paper in a variety of colours
- scissors
- tray
- liquid starch in a cup
- paintbrush
- white paper, board or paper plate

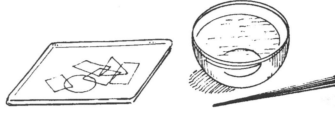

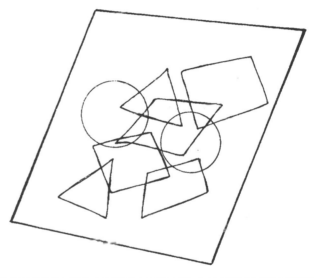

Art process
1. Cut several colours of art tissue paper into squares, triangles, rectangles or any shapes from two to eight cm in size. Place the shapes on a tray.
2. Dip a paintbrush into liquid starch and brush it on the paper, board or paper plate.
3. Press a piece of tissue into the starch.
4. Paint a little more starch over the tissue paper.
5. Continue adding more and more layers of tissue paper and starch, overlapping them to create new colours.
6. The artist may choose to cover all or part of the background.
7. Dry the project completely.

Variations
- Work on wax paper, plastic wrap or any variety of background papers.
- Use clear contact paper and stick the art tissue pieces to the sticky side of the contact paper. Then cover the artwork with another piece of contact paper.
- Substitute thinned PVA glue with starch for a stronger and glossier creation.

 HINT

When the tissue pieces are painted with starch the colour or dye runs out of the paper. Although this is a pretty effect, it can also surprise some artists.

Keep both a wet cloth and a dry cloth handy to clean up sticky fingers.

BASICS

Cut and paste

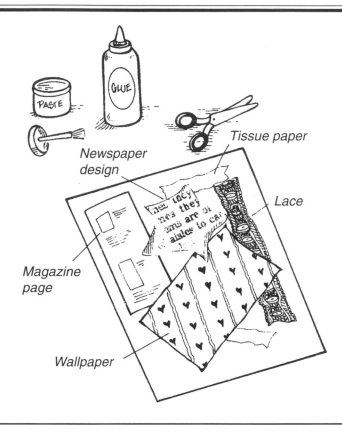

Tissue paper

Newspaper design

Lace

Magazine page

Wallpaper

Materials
- scraps of a variety of papers such as coloured paper, wallpaper, tissue paper or magazine pages
- any pastes or glues
- scissors
- big sheets of paper for background

Art process
1. Using scissors, cut scraps of paper in any desired shape or design.
2. Paste or glue the shape to a larger sheet of paper.
3. Continue cutting and pasting. Designs can be random or realistic.
4. Tearing paper into shapes is an alternative technique to use.
5. The design should dry in a few hours or less.

Variations
- Create a three-dimensional structure, sculpture or construction with paper and paste.
- Make a theme "cut and paste" such as Colours I Love, Wallpapers Only, My Happy Design or Festive Paste-up.
- Add other collage items to the cut and paste project.

BASICS

HINT

This activity provides valuable opportunities for developing creativity and skill-building in young children.

Stick-on stick-upon

Materials
- lots of glue in bottles or in cups with paintbrushes
- masking tape
- clear tape
- stapler
- stickers
- stick-on labels
- collage items such as paper scraps, sewing scraps, glitter, shredded paper, wool or flowers
- background or base materials such as cardboard boxes, plastic jugs, a large ice cream container, newspaper, old posters or paper

Art process
1. Choose a background or base material.
2. Begin gluing and sticking collage items such as cut-up scraps of paper on the base. Completely cover if desired.
3. Dry the project completely.

Variations
- Stick things on a long piece of heavy wool or rope to make a wild and crazy garland to drape around a room.
- Stick things on yourself!
- Make a collage on a cardboard box or plastic jug.
- Save a variety of stick-ons and stick-upons because this activity can be repeated over and over again with different and unique results each time.

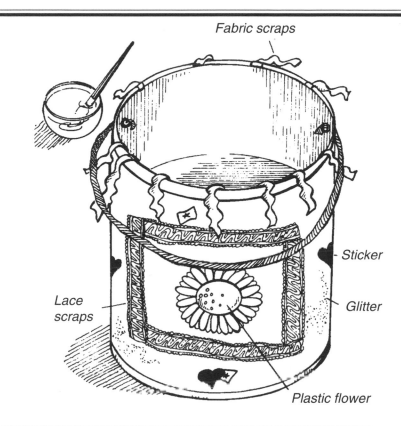

Fabric scraps

Sticker

Lace scraps

Glitter

Plastic flower

COLLAGE

 BASICS

 HINT

Limit the variety of stick-ons provided the first few times the artist explores this activity: young artists sometimes get confused with too many choices. Bring out more materials as the artists develop comfort with the creativity and skill of sticking things together.

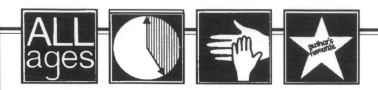

Lace and sew

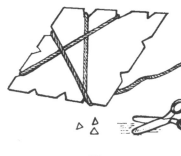

Materials
- board or cardboard cut in squares
- scissors, paper punch
- pre-cut lengths of coloured wool (about 60 cm long)
- masking tape

Art process 1—lace and wrap
1. Cut slits around the edge of a cardboard square.
2. Pull the end of a piece of wool through a slit and then wrap the wool through another slit, criss-crossing the cardboard square as desired.
3. Finish the lacing by tucking the end of wool through a slit and trimming.

Art process 2—"needleless" sewing
1. Punch holes around the edge of a piece of cardboard or a styrofoam tray.
2. Tape the end of a piece of wool with enough masking tape to secure the end of wool and make a needle-like end.
3. Push the taped end of the wool through a hole, pull through and then push the wool through the next hole. Continue "sewing" with the wool until it runs out. Tape the end down.
4. You may sew in more wool if you wish.

Variations
- Colour in the shapes between the wool with felt pens.
- Use embroidery thread instead of wool.
- Sew on old greetings cards.

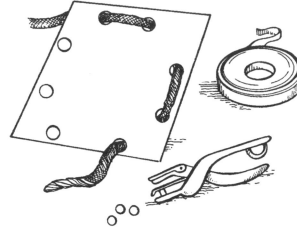

BASICS

HINT

Keep the yarn no longer than 60 cm in length.

If using one of the large plastic darning needles, thread the needle with a doubled 1.4 metre length of yarn, tie both ends in a knot and begin sewing.

Allow space between artists so no one gets poked.

CRAFT

Wood sculpture

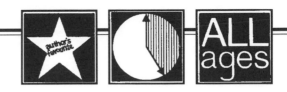

Materials
- scraps of wood (see hints below)
- board, cardboard or square of wood for base, optional
- PVA glue
- decorating items such as ready-mixed paint, glitter, confetti, ribbon, nails, felt pens, nuts and bolts, pieces of straws, pieces of old toys, rubber bands or bits of collage materials

Art process
1. Collect scraps of wood from a secondary school woodwork class or a picture frame shop. Woodwork classes using jig-saws can save curved, puzzle-like and unusually shaped pieces that are creative treasures when making wood sculptures.
2. Work on a base of board or a square of wood if desired.
3. Glue pieces of scrap wood together much like building with blocks. (For quicker and stronger sculptures, an **adult** can handle a glue gun for the artist. This technique must be supervised closely.)
4. Let the sculpture dry overnight.
5. When dry, the artist may choose to further decorate or paint the sculpture.

Variations
- Build a specific object such as a house, bridge or car.
- Combine several sculptures with identical bases to make a large sculpture. Sculptures can be displayed on a wall.

HINT
If a sculpture is top heavy or unbalanced, PVA glue won't hold well. Add some masking tape, rubber bands or other supports until the glue has set. Remove the supports when the project is completely dry.

C O N S T R U C T I O N

BASICS

Junk sculpture

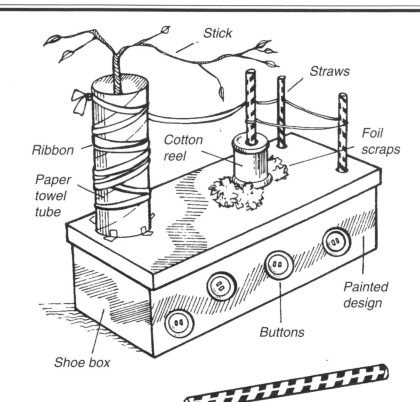

Stick

Straws

Foil scraps

Ribbon

Cotton reel

Paper towel tube

Painted design

Buttons

Shoe box

BASICS

C O N S T R U C T I O N

HINT Save lots and lots of interesting "junk" and this sculpture activity can be repeated over and over without the same results!

As always, a glue gun is an alternative for sturdy quick gluing, but requires one-to-one adult supervision.

Materials
- all kinds of recycled, reusable "junk", such as paper tubes, egg cartons, pieces of toys, bits of fabric and ribbon, corks, buttons, cotton reels, wood scraps, foil or cardboard boxes
- PVA glue
- something for a base, such as board, cardboard, heavy paper or a styrofoam tray
- ready-mixed paints and brushes, optional

Art process
1. Glue items together to make a three-dimensional sculpture. Sculptures can be tall, short, wide or tiny but should come up off the base and have dimension.
2. When the sculpture is dry, other decorations or paints can be added.

Variations
- Choose one type of junk and make a sculpture such as a paper tube sculpture, egg carton sculpture, stones and sticks sculpture or a wood scrap sculpture.
- Create a theme sculpture, such as Playground Rubbish Sculpture, Walk in the Woods Sculpture, Toys and Play Sculpture or a Happiness Sculpture.

Fried paper plates

Materials
- electric frying pan completely lined with aluminium foil
- paper plates
- old crayon stubs, peeled
- old cheese grater
- wooden craft stick
- newspaper to cover work surface
- oven gloves

Art process
1. **Adult** plugs in and turns on the electric frying pan to 150ºF (90ºC) or warm setting.
2. Slip a paper plate into the warm frying pan.
3. Wear oven gloves to protect hands. Drop bits of old crayon stubs on to the plate.
4. Add shaved bits of crayon to the plate.
5. Push some of the crayon around with the end of a wooden craft stick to enhance the design.
6. **Adult** removes the plate from the frying pan when the melted design is complete.

Variation
- Use a warming tray instead of an electric frying pan to melt the crayon.

HINT

To remove the plate from the pan easily, attach a tab of masking tape to the edge of the paper plate before placing it in the pan. Use the tab to lift the plate from the pan.

If the plate tends to spin around in the pan as the artist is working, place a loop of masking tape on the back of the paper plate before placing it in the pan.

DRAWING

Baby oil drawing

Materials
- good quality paper, any colour
- cotton wool balls, cotton swabs or a paintbrush
- baby oil in small dish
- newspaper-covered table

Art process
1. Dip the cotton wool ball into the dish of baby oil.
2. Draw a design on the paper with the oil-soaked cotton wool ball.
3. Dip other drawing tools such as a cotton swab or a paintbrush into the oil and draw on the paper.
4. After the oil soaks into the paper, hold the drawing up to the light and look at the transparent design.

Variations
- Use watercolours to paint a design on the baby oil drawing and observe how the oil resists the paint.
- Use crayons to draw on the paper and then rub the drawing with baby oil on a cotton wool ball to enrich the colours.

 HINT

To prevent tipping dishes of oil during use, stick a loop of wide masking tape to the bottom of the dish, and press dish to table surface.

Each drawing may take many cotton balls to complete since many young artists are apt to explore the delightful qualities of the soft, oily cotton ball.

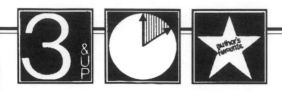

Glossy pen paper

Materials
- heavy, glossy paper (available from scrap bin in print shops)
- felt pens
- paintbrush and cup of water, optional

Art process
1. Visit a print shop and collect heavy, glossy paper used to print posters and colour brochures.
2. Draw on the paper with felt pens, feeling the pens slide as the colours glide about.
3. If desired, dip a paintbrush into clear water and smudge and blur the pen marks like "paint-with-water".

Variations
- First dampen the paper with a sponge and then draw with felt pens on the wet, glossy paper.
- Experiment with felt pens on other unusual types of paper.

 HINT *Ask a local printer to save a box of papers in all colours, textures and sizes. Printers are valuable sources for free and unusual paper for children, parents or teachers.*

Fabric pen stencil

Materials
- small squares of clear contact paper
- white cotton fabric such as a shirt, sheet, pillowcase or tablecloth
- fabric pens (available at fabric stores and from school supply catalogues)
- scissors
- masking tape

Art process
1. Spread the fabric out on the table. Tape down corners to keep fabric from slipping.
2. Cut shapes or designs from the clear contact paper.
3. Peel the backing from each shape or design and press on to the fabric.
4. Draw, colour, trace or scribble over the fabric and the clear contact shapes. Work until the design is complete.
5. Peel the contact paper off the fabric. White areas will appear where the contact paper used to be.

Variations
- Cut letters and spell names or greetings on the fabric.
- Make planned designs and patterns for your project.
- Cut out a stencil for a design, and use the hole left from the cut-out for an opposite design.
- Stick pieces of tape to heavy paper, colour over them and then remove the tape.

HINT

Although kids can peel the backing off the contact paper pretty well, they sometimes need help controlling the sticky unruliness of the contact paper.

Have some small scraps of fabric and pieces of contact paper available to practise the concept of colouring over a stencil on fabric before using the shirt or pillowcase.

DRAWING

Textured table

Materials
- table
- large sheet of thin paper in any light colour
- peeled jumbo crayon
- items to provide textures, such as wool, sandpaper, paper shapes, fabric scraps, coins, confetti, glitter or paper-clips
- masking tape

Art process
1. Spread a variety of the texture items all around the surface of a table. These items should be fairly flat and not too pointy or sharp.
2. Place a large sheet of lining paper over the table like a tablecloth. Tape the corners and sides of the paper to the table to prevent slipping.
3. Rub the jumbo peeled crayons on their sides back and forth all over the lining paper. Many surprise textures will appear.
4. Feel the top of the paper with hands to be sure all the textures have been rubbed with crayon.
5. Leave the textured design on the table for a fancy table covering or remove it for a wall decoration, wrapping paper or other decorative use.

Variation
- Make small rubbings on a tray with one sheet of paper. It's fun to hide items under the paper and have a friend do the rubbing to discover what is hidden beneath the paper.

HINT *Some young artists are only beginning to understand the concept of crayon rubbings, using the sides of the crayons or finding hidden textures. This activity gives them a chance to experience rubbings with large arm movements and stable paper.*

Fingerpaint leaves

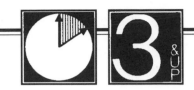

Materials
- big, autumn leaves
- fingerpaint in containers
- big piece of paper or newsprint
- newspaper-covered work surface
- soapy water in bucket for clean-up
- towel

Art process
1. Collect big, autumn leaves (such as horse chestnut leaves) that are still supple.
2. Place a leaf on the newspaper.
3. Dip fingers in the fingerpaint and smooth and smear paint all over one side of the leaf.
4. Use fingers to draw designs into the paint on the leaf.
5. Wash and dry hands.
6. Place a sheet of newsprint over the leaf and with gentle pressure pat the paper on to the painted leaf.
7. Peel the paper away from the leaf or peel the leaf off the paper.
8. An imprint from the fingerpainting and the leaf will be transferred to the paper.

Variation
- Place leaves under paper and rub with peeled crayons to create leaf rubbings

HINT *A simple finger paint recipe is to mix four tablespoons of liquid starch and a tablespoon of powdered or ready-mixed paint. Stir with a stick and use as fingerpaint. The measurements are not strict so experiment with colour, intensity and thickness.*

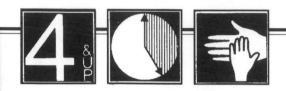

Rolling pattern

Materials
- cardboard
- fresh leaves
- PVA glue
- ready-mixed paint
- baking tray
- print roller, child's rolling pin or dowel
- absorbent paper
- spoon

Art process
1. Arrange the leaves in a design on the cardboard.
2. Glue the leaves to the cardboard and let dry.
3. Place a spoonful of paint on a baking tray. Move the roller though the paint until the roller is evenly coated.
4. Roll the paint on the leaves.
5. Place a piece of paper on top of the leaves.
6. Rub the paper with clean, dry hands.
7. Peel off the paper and see the raised veins and edges of the leaves imprinted on the paper.
8. Make several prints from the same painting.

Variations
- The same technique can be used with wire mesh, lace or netting instead of leaves.
- Different colours of paint can be mixed on the baking tray for a swirl of colours on the leaves.

HINT

Moist, fresh leaves work the best.

Print rollers and are available from art supply shops and school supply catalogues.

Styrofoam print

Materials
- styrofoam grocery tray (sides trimmed away) or polystyrene sheet, cut into quarters (available from art shops or school supply catalogues)
- ready-mixed paint on a baking tray
- pencil
- print roller or child's rolling pin
- typing paper
- covered work surface

Art process
1. Press a pencil firmly into the styrofoam to make a design (see hints).
2. Roll a print roller through the paint on the baking tray. Roll the roller across the styrofoam design.
3. Place a piece of paper on top of the styrofoam and use gentle pressure with the fingers to deliver an even painting.
4. Peel away the paper. Dry the painting.
5. Use the same colour, a new colour or several new colours of paint to make another print. Repaint the styrofoam each time a print is made.

Variation
- Make several prints of the same design using several different colours of paper. Cut the papers in strips, reassemble the design using different coloured strips and glue on to a background paper.

HINT *Any lines or shapes pressed into the styrofoam will show as white on the white paper; all the raised areas of the styrofoam will print the colour of the paint being used. Some artists like to think of leaving the design "tall" and the background pushed down. This is a more abstract, advanced print but many children understand it perfectly.*

P
A
I
N
T
I
N
G

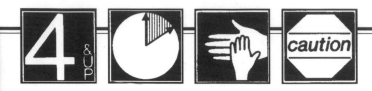

Sponge wrap

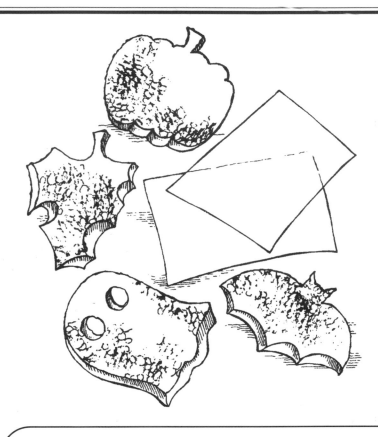

Materials
- sponges
- scissors
- several colours of paste food colouring mixed with a little water on a styrofoam meat tray
- sheets of white tissue paper
- paintbrush

Art process
1. **Adult** helps cut sponges into autumn shapes such as leaves, apples, pears or pumpkins.
2. Place thinned paste food colourings in meat trays. Keep a paintbrush handy to dab on sponges for more coverage.
3. Dip a sponge into the colouring and then press it on to an open sheet of white tissue paper. The sponge will tend to stick and lift the paper, so carefully pull the sponge and paper apart.
4. Dip other sponges into the colourings, watching to see the different designs left from different shapes.
5. Print with sponges until the paper is filled with a desired design.
6. Dry the tissue paper completely. Fold and save the paper or use immediately for wrapping paper.

Variation
- Print with other items such as cork, parts of toys, blocks or biscuit cutters

HINT

If wrapping paper gets wet later, the design can rub off on clothing or hands so try to keep it dry. For "stain-proof" colouring, buy fabric or paper dye from an art shop. It is slightly expensive, but it goes further, comes in a larger variety of colours and lasts longer than paste food colouring.

Chalky leaf spatter

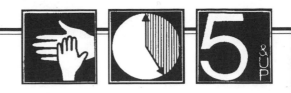

Materials

- nail-brush
- wire screen, stapled to old picture frame
- thin ready-mixed paint in a bowl
- chalk
- paper
- pressed leaves, flowers or any flat items
- large cardboard box with one side cut out
- tape
- smock or old shirt

Art process

1. Place a sheet of paper inside the box and tape the edges down so it won't wiggle.
2. Place leaves, flowers, grasses or paper shapes on the paper.
3. Place the wire screen in the frame over the paper. The screen should be several centimetres above the paper.
4. Dip the nail-brush into the paint.
5. Rub the paint-filled brush many times across the screen. If the brush is loaded with paint, the spatter drops will be big and coarse.
6. Next take a piece of chalk and rub it across the screen. Bits of chalk will fall through the screen and land in the wet paint adding additional colour to the spatter design. If the screen gets clogged with paint, rinse it clean, shake it dry and then add the chalk.
7. Dry the completed artwork. Remove the leaves and other objects or stencils.

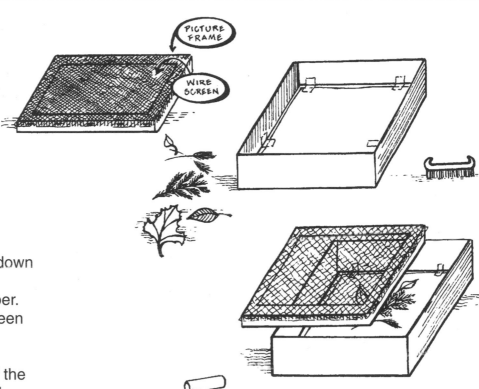

PICTURE FRAME

WIRE SCREEN

HINT *The box keeps the spattering paint within a boundary. Be sure to cover the child with an old shirt too.*

P A I N T I N G

Nature garden

C L A Y

Materials
- playdough
- heavy paper plate
- autumn seeds and weeds such as twigs, nuts, thistles, pine cones, seed pods, leaves, stones, fresh or dry flowers

Art process
1. Place a ball of playdough in the centre of the paper plate. Spread the playdough out to the sides. Add more playdough to fill the plate completely with a thick layer.
2. Stick leaves, flowers and other found objects from outdoors into the playdough to make a "garden". Some leaves or weeds can also lie flat in the playdough.
3. When the design is complete, place it in the centre of a table or on a shelf to enjoy.

Variations
- Make a miniature garden in an egg carton cup or a small paper plate.
- Add small figures or toys to the garden.
- Add a small mirror to the garden and partially bury it with playdough to simulate a pond.

HINT *Collect and save things all year long for the nature garden.*

Paper bag sculpture

Materials
- paper bags, any size
- newspaper for stuffing
- strips of newspaper
- flour and water paste from hardware shop in bowl (or make a homemade paste from recipe below)
- ready-mixed paints in cups
- paintbrushes
- covered work area
- homemade paste for papier mâché:
  Stir 300 g of flour into 690 ml of cold water in a pan. Cook the mixture over low heat until it thickens and has a creamy paste-like consistency. Add more water if it is too thick. Cool the paste and add a few drops of peppermint oil. Use the paste to coat strips of paper.

Art process
1. Fill a paper bag with wads of newspaper and shape the bag into any form for the base of the sculpture.
2. Dip strips of newspaper into papier mâché paste and wrap around the paper bag base. Continue using the strips to form details for the sculpture such as arms, tail or handles.
3. Squeeze the paste from each strip before placing it on the sculpture. Young artists like to pull the strip between their fingers to wring out excess paste.
4. Dry the sculpture overnight. In moist weather, complete drying can take up to two days.
5. When completely dry, paint the sculpture with ready-mixed paints.

HINT

Paper bags are easier than balloons for young children to control during their first attempt at papier mâché. Keep in mind that almost anything can be covered with papier mâché including a cardboard box, milk carton or meat tray.

Flour and water paste and wallpaper paste work equally well and can be purchased from a hardware shop.

Nature collage

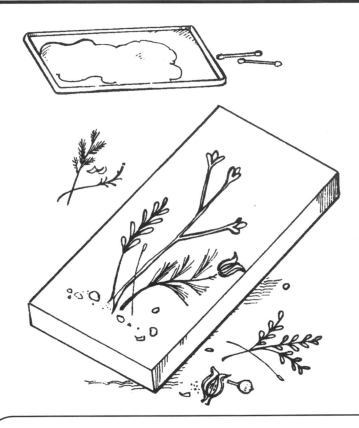

Materials
- PVA glue
- styrofoam grocery tray
- nature items such as pebbles, bark, leaves, nuts, pine needles, pine cones, seeds, wood shavings, shells, seed pods or dried weeds
- piece of wood for base
- craft stick
- cotton swab

Art process
1. Squeeze a puddle of glue in the middle of a styrofoam meat tray.
2. Select an item from nature and arrange it on the base piece of wood. Dab the item with glue from a craft stick or cotton swab. The artist may also choose to dip the item in the puddle of glue.
3. Now stick the item on the base piece of wood.
4. Add more bits of things from nature and attach them to the piece of wood with glue.
5. When satisfied with the arrangement, allow the collage to dry overnight or over several days.

Variations
- Using felt pen or paint, make areas of colour on the wood base and then glue the nature items into the colour design.
- Nature collage can be made on fabric-covered wood, a paper plate, cardboard, plaster of Paris in a pie plate or any number of other backgrounds.

HINT

As an alternative to PVA glue, a glue gun provides immediate, strong, long-lasting results. Constant one-to-one adult supervision is necessary when using a glue gun.

COLLAGE

Mixed-up magazine

Materials
- pre-cut magazine pictures
- paper, cardboard, box lid or paper plate for the base
- paste or glue
- felt pens or crayons

Art process
1. Choose a magazine picture.
2. Cut an important part from the picture such as the head of a dog, a baby's foot or a glass of milk. Glue it to the base of the paper or cardboard.
3. Choose another unrelated magazine picture and add a part of that picture to the first part. The idea is to make a silly picture combining unrelated parts such as the head of a dog, the body of a boy, two feet made of bananas and so on.
4. When a substantially silly picture is complete, dry for an hour or so.

Variations
- Glue a part from a magazine picture on a piece of paper. Give the artist the challenge of adding other parts to the pre-glued piece.
- Be creative. Imagine a spaghetti face for a boy with a tree trunk body sleeping on a bed of clouds. Imagine other ideas while flipping through magazines collecting pictures.

 HINT *Young artists find "mixed-up magazine" incredibly funny. Be prepared for some very silly artists who may not want to complete one full picture but make many silly scenes. This project is truly enjoyable.*

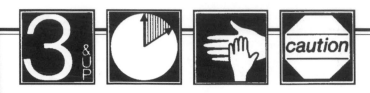

Glue-over

Materials
- styrofoam grocery tray
- scissors
- felt pens
- paintbrush
- PVA glue in a cup

Art process
1. **Adult** cuts a shape or piece from a styrofoam meat tray.
2. Draw on the styrofoam piece with felt pens using a wide variety of colours, completely covering the surface.
3. Dry the artwork.
4. Paint PVA glue over the entire surface of the coloured piece.
5. Dry the glue completely to produce a slick sealed surface that brightens and enhances the colours underneath.

Variations
- Use the glue-over as an ornament, to hang from a mobile or as a piece of artwork to hang on the wall.
- If hanging the glue-over on the wall, use a pencil to poke a small hole in the styrofoam and insert a bit of wool. You may also tape a paper-clip to the back of the design.

HINT *Glue-overs can be made very small or very large depending on the artist's choice, plan or desire.*

Branch weaving

Materials
- tree branch with at least three smaller branches shooting out
- wool in many colours and textures
- unspun sheep's wool
- nature items such as long grasses, weeds, feathers or corn husks
- strips of fabric, ribbon and other strings or cords
- scissors

Art process
1. **Adult** helps the artist start at the top or the bottom of one small branch by looping some wool around the branch to get the project started.
2. Wrap yarn around smaller branches to make a base of wool moving up or down the branches.
3. Weave other wool, unspun sheep's wool, grasses, fabric strips or any intriguing items into the wool base. Random weaving and wrapping is also effective.
4. Wrap and weave until the branch weaving is complete.

Variation
- Nail or glue strips of thin wood into a frame or box shape. Wrap and weave wool on the wood base.

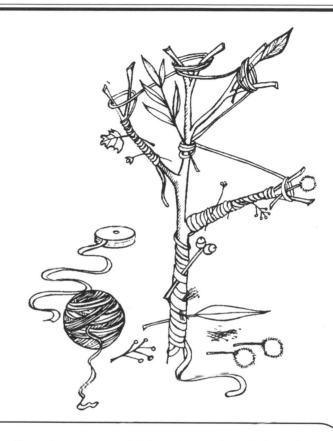

HINT *Keep the wool about 60 cm in length so it doesn't get out of control. When the wool is too short it can be frustrating and when it is too long it gets tangled. More wool can always be added as each piece is used up.*

Puzzle paste

Materials
- magazine picture or child's drawing
- scissors
- posterboard or heavy paper larger than the picture
- glue

Art process
1. Choose a magazine picture or a child's drawing for the puzzle picture.
2. Cut the picture or drawing into large simple shapes or strips.
3. Place the pieces of the picture on the posterboard in the same order as the original picture.
4. Pick up one piece, put glue on the back and glue it to the posterboard.
5. The second piece should be glued in order, but leave a space between pieces. Continue gluing the pieces to the posterboard remembering to leave spaces between each piece.
6. When all the pieces are glued in place, the picture will be spread out and appear to be an optical illusion because of the spaces.
7. Dry the picture for an hour.

Variation
- Glue the full, uncut picture to the posterboard. When dry, take scissors and cut it into strips or large, simple pieces. This cut-apart picture becomes a puzzle and can be kept in a box or an envelope to be played with as any puzzle.

HINT

If a child's drawing is used, be sure the child has agreed to having his drawing cut apart and understands that it will not go back together.

Finger puppets

Materials
- felt pieces, about 8 cm x 5 cm
- sewing machine
- fabric scraps, buttons, sequins, feathers and craft eyes
- PVA glue or craft glue
- felt pens
- scissors

Art process
1. **Adult** cuts two pieces of felt, about 8 cm long by 5 cm wide.
2. Place one piece of felt on top of the other and sew a zigzag stitch around the felt, making the top rounded and leaving the bottom open for finger access.
3. Have the artist glue any materials to the base to create an animal, person or character. Use felt pens to add features.
4. Dry the puppet.
5. Make up stories, plays or dances using the finger puppets as the main characters.

Variations
- Cut the fingers off an old glove and make each glove segment a puppet.
- Make puppets from a favourite book and act out the story with the puppets.
- Sing a song with the finger puppets.

 HINT *Some young artists may be able to sew the base together with supervision.*

Measurements can be adjusted for size.

Paper strip sculpture

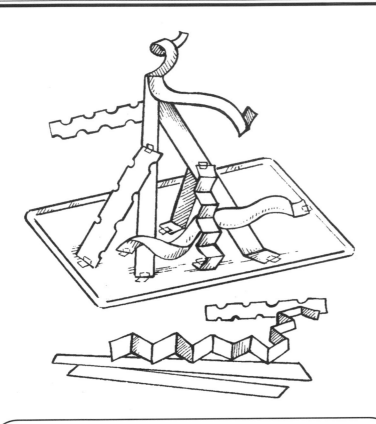

HINT *Paper strip sculpture is interesting because of the interaction of paper strips; it does not need to "be" anything or look like anything.*

Materials
- styrofoam grocery tray for a base
- strips of sugar paper
- tape, glue and stapler
- paper punch
- scissors

Art process
1. Attach one end of a paper strip to the grocery tray base using a stapler or tape.
2. Secure another strip to the first one with tape, glue or a stapler.
3. Continue adding strips of paper to the base or to the other strips of paper. Strips can be pleated, folded, connected, cut, paper-punched or fringed with scissors. Let the artists use their imagination!
4. The goal is to create a three-dimensional paper sculpture. Once this has been accomplished and the artist is satisfied with the art, the project is complete.
5. Dry the project completely if glue was used.

Variations
- Add other items to the sculpture such as paper shapes, glitter, confetti, magazine pictures or strips. The artists may also sew and tie pieces of wool to their sculpture.
- Use other materials to complete this project. Choose items such as board or wood for the base. Use other types of paper such as computer paper or wrapping paper to create the sculpture. Join the paper together with stickers or paper-clips.

Dark sugar chalk

Materials
- coloured chalk
- black paper or board
- 70 g sugar dissolved in 230 ml water
- cotton wool balls, optional

Art process
1. Soak chalk sticks in the sugar-water for five to ten minutes. This adds brilliance to the colour and helps resist smudging.
2. Draw on the black paper with the sugar chalk. Lines can be bold and bright or light and blurry.
3. Brush chalk marks with cotton wool balls as an optional art technique.

Variations
- Make a spooky autumn drawing. The black background will make the colours seem to glow.
- Use other colours and different textures of paper.
- Paint the paper with a mixture of evaporated milk and liquid starch. Draw on the wet paper for a sparkling effect.

D R A W I N G

HINT *Chalk is inherently smudgy, but the sugar-water mixture will help reduce smudging.*

Handful scribble

Materials
- handful of crayons all the same length
- rubber band
- paper
- masking tape
- music, optional

Art process
1. Tape a piece of paper to the table to prevent slipping.
2. Bundle a handful of crayons (three or more) with a rubber band. Tap the bundle on the paper to make sure all the crayon points are even.
3. Scribble and colour on the paper watching the rainbow effect of many crayons making the same marks.
4. Add music to the scribbling and make marks or strokes that show how the music feels. Remove tape and turn the paper adding more musical scribbles.

Variations
- Use the scribbled paper for a crayon-resist by painting over the design with a wash of blue, black or purple paint.
- Use the artwork for wrapping paper.
- Use the scribbled paper as a background for a framed picture or as the background for a finger painting.

HINT

Artists become very energetic when music is added. Using large sheets of paper on the floor or wall can accommodate "dancing arms".

Sponge chalk

Materials
- large, flat wet sponge
- coloured chalk
- paper

Art process
1. Draw freely on the wet sponge with chalk.
2. Press the sponge on to paper to transfer a print of the sponge design to the paper.

Variation
- Grind, crush or grate chalk into a dish. Dip pieces of wet sponge into the chalk and dab them on the paper.

HINT *Chalk breaks often which is perfectly chalk-like. Just use the small pieces until they are too small to hold. Save the tiny pieces to grind or crush into powder for other art projects.*

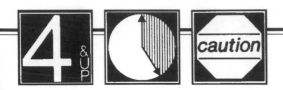

Spider's web

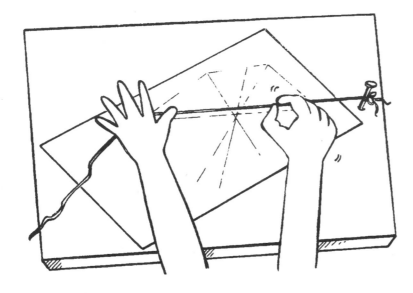

Materials
- square of plywood, about 1 metre square
- pencils, crayons and felt pens
- several nails
- hammer
- heavy string
- chalk
- paper
- masking tape

Art process
1. Hammer a nail near the top edge of the plywood square. Be careful not to hammer through the wood and into the floor or table.
2. Tie one end of a 60–100 cm piece of heavy string to the nail.
3. Place a sheet of paper in the centre of the board.
4. Rub chalk back and forth on the string until the string is coated.
5. Hold the loose end of the string with one hand and pull it very tight over the paper. Use the other hand to lift the centre of the string then let go, snapping it against the paper. A puff of chalk will snap against the paper and leave a soft line.
6. Turn the paper. Rub more chalk on the string. Snap it to release another line that crosses the first.
7. Continue turning the paper and snapping chalk lines until the design begins to resemble the framework of a spider's web.
8. When ready, move the paper to a table and add the connecting spider's web lines with chalk, pencil, felt pen or crayon. Add a spider too, if desired.

HINT

White chalk on black paper is effective but various colours on white or black paper are pretty too.

When the chalk sticks are rubbed back and forth, the string scores the chalk and the stick breaks easily. Use these small pieces to continue rubbing the string. When pieces are too small to handle, save them for other art activities where chalk is crushed or grated.

Bear in mind some artists will create a design instead of a spider's web.

Buttermilk chalk screen

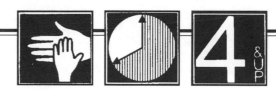

Materials

- wire mesh screen (stapled to back of old picture frame)
- coloured chalk
- buttermilk in cup
- paintbrush
- paper
- covered work area

Buttermilk

Art process

1. Place a sheet of paper on the work area.
2. Paint the paper with buttermilk.
3. Place the picture frame with screen on the paper. The wire mesh should be on the back of the frame and up off the paper.
4. Rub coloured chalk back and forth over the screen so that powdered bits of chalk fall into the buttermilk on the paper beneath.
5. Try different colours of chalk and different areas of the screen.
6. Lift the frame and screen and watch the effect of the chalk absorbing the buttermilk on the paper as a sparkling result occurs.
7. Dry the chalk art completely.

Variations

- This project can be repeated with paint spattered through the screen from a nail-brush or toothbrush.
- Paint the paper with a combination of liquid starch and evaporated milk instead of buttermilk for a similar effect.
- Place paper shapes or stencils on the paper before rubbing the chalk through the screen. After chalking, remove the stencils and see the design left on the paper.

HINT

Be sure the screen is securely stapled to the back of the frame. Reinforce with duct tape if necessary. Young artists tend to press hard on the screen and it can tear away from the frame if not secure.

If you don't have buttermilk, add a 1/2 teaspoon of vinegar to ordinary milk and let it sit for five minutes. Do not drink.

Mystery paint

HINT *Very young artists can be sceptical about painting something they can't see, but they soon catch on to the fun.*

Materials
- 4 tablespoons bicarbonate of soda
- 4 tablespoons water
- cup to mix bicarbonate of soda and water
- cotton swabs
- sheet of white paper
- watercolour paint
- paintbrush

Art process
1. Dissolve the bicarbonate of soda and water in a cup.
2. Dip the cotton swab in the mixture and paint an invisible picture on the white paper.
3. Dry the artwork completely.
4. Brush the watercolour paint over the paper to reveal the mystery picture.

Variations
- Create a secret picture for a friend to reveal with watercolour paint.
- Create a secret message for a friend.
- Add crayon to the mystery painting and then brush with watercolour paint for a mystery wax-resist.

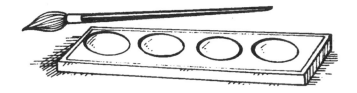

Fingerprints

Materials

- choose one of the following for the colour
  - food colouring (dip fingers in liquid placed in a jar lid)
  - felt pens (colour fingertips)
  - ink pads (press fingertips on to pad)
  - ready-mixed paints (press fingertips on pads of damp paper towels and paint)
- paper
- fine tip felt pens for adding features
- soapy water in bucket and towel for clean-up

Art process

1. First choose one of the colouring methods.
2. Colour a favourite finger or thumb with the chosen colour.
3. Press the coloured finger on to the paper. The artist may press several times before re-colouring.
4. Dry the artwork.
5. Add details to the fingerprints with fine felt tip markers such as features, hats, ears or feet.

Variation

- Draw a picture with a crayon and then add fingerprints to enhance the drawing. Some examples include: fingerprint blossoms in a crayon tree or flower pot, fingerprint hair on a funny face or fingerprint insects on a crayon branch.

HINT *Some artists enjoy messy hands and fingers; other artists find the mess almost unbearable. Some of the aversion is due to a developmentally recognized correlation between messy hands and potty training. The aversion usually passes and artists become comfortable with messy hands and fingers again as they get older.*

PAINTING

Tilt prints

Materials
- items to use for printing such as small balls, nuts and bolts, marbles, pieces of small toys or other small rolling items
- several colours of ready-mixed paint in cups with spoons
- shallow baking pan
- paper to fit pan
- bowl of soapy water and towels

Art process
1. Place the paper in the baking pan.
2. Select some rolling items such as nuts and bolts or marbles.
3. With a spoon drop puddles of paint on the paper.
4. Drop the rolling items into the pan and tilt the pan around, rolling them through the paint and making designs on the paper.
5. Dry the completed artwork.
6. To wash up, drop painted items into the bowl of soapy water and wash. Wash hands too. Dry the items and hands.

Variations
- Use a round cake pan with a paper plate in it.
- Put a puddle of paint on an incline board covered with paper and roll the same items through the paint down the board.
- Roll hard-boiled eggs through paint puddles in a washing-up bowl to decorate the eggs.

HINT

Experiment with different items to roll. Some items make amazing prints that surprise everyone.

Items used for tilt prints may not come completely clean.

Chalk paint

Materials

- cheese grater
- coloured chalk
- greaseproof paper square
- muffin tin
- cotton buds
- water in small dishes
- paper

Art process

1. **Adult** helps the artist grate coloured chalk on to a square of greaseproof paper. Shake the chalk gratings into a muffin cup.
2. Dip a cotton bud into water and then into the powdered, grated chalk and paint on the paper freely.
3. Dry the project completely.

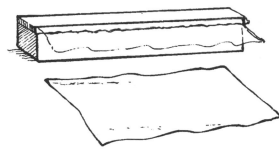

Variations

- Put powdered paint in separate small containers. Paint by dipping cotton buds in the water and then into the powdered paint.
- Experiment with other drawing or painting tools such as a paintbrush, feather or finger.
- Work on paper that has been pre-moistened with water, buttermilk or a mixture of liquid starch and evaporated milk.

HINT

For a fine powdered chalk, crush the chalk with a hammer or stone instead of using a cheese grater.

Art chalk works better than the dustless chalkboard variety of chalk.

Shoe polish leaves

Materials
- supple autumn leaves
- shoe polish in bottle with applicator (variety of colours)
- variety of papers
- covered work surface
- extra sheets of newsprint
- bucket of soapy water
- nail-brush
- towel

Art process
1. Collect fresh autumn leaves in a variety of shapes and sizes.
2. Place a leaf on a piece of newsprint, face down.
3. Dab shoe polish over the back surface of the leaf.
4. Select a piece of paper and lay it gently on the shoe-polished leaf. Press and pat the paper gently over the leaf.
5. Peel the paper and leaf apart revealing a shoe polish leaf print on the paper.
6. Select another leaf, change polish colours or make a print on a new sheet of newsprint.

Variations
- Place a leaf on a sheet of paper. Dab shoe polish around the edges of the leaf, brushing out from the edges on to the paper. Remove the leaf and a stencil design will be left.
- Experiment with patterns and designs, types of paper and colours of shoe polish.

HINT

Shoe polish stains hands and fingernails. Have a soapy bucket of water close by with nail-brush and towel for clean-up.

Shoe polish leaf prints show the veins and features of leaves in detail.

Cheesy-pumpkin

Materials
- 400 g grated cheddar cheese
- 50 g flour
- 2 tablespoons mayonnaise
- bowl
- clean work surface
- square of greaseproof paper
- clean hands
- plastic knife, toothpick and other kitchen tools

Art process
1. With adult help, mix the cheese, flour and mayonnaise in a bowl with clean hands. Squeeze and blend the ingredients until the consistency of dough. Add more flour if the dough is too sticky and more cheese or mayonnaise if the dough is too stiff or dry.
2. Place a ball of cheese dough on a square of greaseproof paper on a clean work surface.
3. Mould, pat and sculpt the cheese dough into a flattened oval or circle resembling a pumpkin.
4. With a plastic knife or other kitchen tool, dig or cut away holes for the pumpkin's face.
5. Leave the face on the greaseproof paper square and save in the fridge to eat later.
6. Make as many cheese sculptures or faces as desired.

Variation
- Use white cheese and make little cheese ghosts with faces.

 HINT | *When using food for art, be sure the project is part of a meal or nutritious snack.*

Pumpkin face mystery

Materials
- scrap black paper
- box or bucket
- orange paper
- glue or tape
- scissors

Art process
1. With adult help, cut black paper into strange or realistic shapes to suggest a mouth, eyes, nose or other facial feature. Shapes can be very large or very small.
2. Place these black scrap features into a box or bucket.
3. With adult help, cut orange paper into circles and ovals of all sizes ranging from very large to very small.
4. Place a few orange circles or ovals on the floor.
5. Reach into the box and pull out a black scrap. Place the scrap on the circle or oval to begin building a face for a pumpkin. Features can be silly, realistic, scary or any style desired. The fun of this project is the mystery of how the pumpkin face will turn out since it is created by drawing the features randomly from a box.
6. Make several different pumpkin faces. Play by changing the features around to see what different expressions and personalities can be created.
7. If desired, tape or glue the features in place and hang the completed pumpkin faces in a window, on a wall or as a doorway decoration.

HINT *Some artists will choose to create random designs instead of pumpkin faces. Allow for creativity and imagination.*

COLLAGE

Impress wall pot

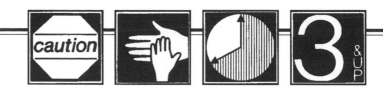

Materials
- salt, flour and water to make baker's clay (see recipe below)
- measuring jug
- rolling pin
- other kitchen tools such as a spatula or knife
- items to press into clay such as toys, buttons, fork, nuts, bolt or a pencil
- baking tray
- oven preheated to 300ºF (150ºC)
- wool
- collection of dried weeds and grasses from outside

Art process
1. Make the baker's clay by hand mixing one part salt, four parts flour and one-and-a-half parts water in a bowl. Knead the mixture for five minutes until soft and pliable.
2. Place two balls of clay on the table and roll each one out flat. Place one piece on a baking tray.
3. Decorate the clay by pressing toys or other items into it.
4. Carefully lift the decorated piece and lay it on top of the plain piece. Lift the top edge of the top piece of clay to create an envelope-like opening. Press the rest of the edges together with a fork or pinch with the fingers. Poke two little holes in the top of the clay envelope for hanging with wool later.
5. Bake the completed pots in a 300ºF (150ºC) oven for about an hour or two or until nicely browned and hard all the way through.
6. **Adult** removes the pots from the oven.

7. When cool, stick bits of weeds, dried flowers or grasses into the opening of the "envelope".
8. Add a wool piece through the holes in the top of the design and hang the finished pot on the wall as a decoration.

HINT — Experiment and explore with various doughs and clays before attempting to make this project. Many artists need to know how each dough acts before making a craft or sculpture.

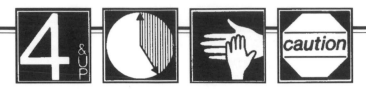

Weaving board

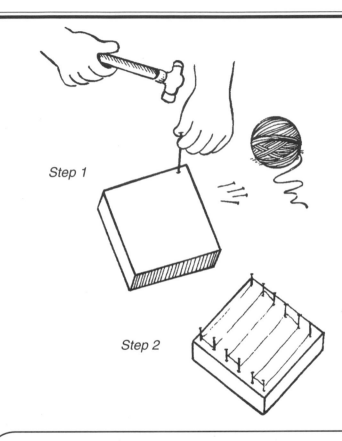

Step 1

Step 2

Materials
- flat scrap of wood for weaving board
- finishing nails (no head)
- hammer
- heavy string
- wool
- other weaving materials such as strips of fabric, ribbon, dry grass, sewing trim, crepe paper or raffia
- scissors

Art process
1. **Adult** helps hammer nails into two edges of a flat board from 0.5–2.5 cm apart. Help the artist hammer nails so they are in tight and firm but not poking through the other side of the wood.
2. Help the artist wrap heavy string back and forth from one side of the board to the other. Start with the first nail and end with the last nail. Tie the string securely. The heavy string is called the warp.
3. With colourful wool, ribbon, strips of fabric or other long material (called the weft), push the weft string under and over the heavy warp strings. There is no need to weave in a specific style.
4. Change colours and materials, if desired, and continue weaving in any way, form or pattern. Tuck in loose ends or tie the end of one loose end to the beginning of the next.
5. Weave until the warp strings are completely full.
6. Remove the warp from the nails when complete or leave the artwork on the weaving board for display.

HINT

Allow for exploration with many weaving materials and activities. Then demonstrate the over-under technique and the over-two-under-one pattern. Because the artist is experienced, the demonstrations will make more sense.

Stocking mask

Materials
- nylon stocking or tights
- wire coat hanger
- ribbon or rubber band
- fabric scraps, buttons, wool, paper-clips, beads, old jewellery or earrings or rug scraps to make the face
- glue or needle and thread

Art process
1. **Adult** helps round out a wire coat hanger with the hook at the base, to resemble the shape of a hand mirror.
2. Cut the stocking as shown in the illustration. Two masks can be made from each leg of a pair of tights.
3. Pull the section of stocking with the foot attached over the coat hanger and secure with a ribbon or rubber band at the hooked end of the hanger. If the thigh section of the stocking is used, both the top and the base must be tied around the hanger.
4. Make a face on the stretched stocking with scraps, buttons, wool or other decorative items. Glue or hand stitch the pieces on the stocking mask.
5. When dry, hold the stocking mask up and speak or act while hiding behind it.

Variation
- If a wire hanger is not available, an adult can cut an oval of heavy cardboard into a mask shape and cut out the middle for the stocking face. This material may not be as strong as the wire hanger so the stocking may need to be cut into a single layer, stretched and stapled or taped to the cardboard.

HINT

Be aware that very young children can be frightened of masks because they have not yet learned to separate fantasy and reality.

Masks can make a shy child daring, a gentle child rough, a bold child quiet or a rough child gentle thereby revealing any number of secrets and surprises.

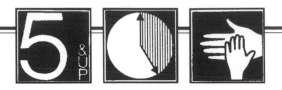

Ghost tree

Glue

Open

 HINT *Paper can be sewn on a sewing machine instead of using glue. Use a long stitch or a zigzag stitch.*

Materials
- tree branch
- coffee tin filled with sand
- coloured paper
- heavy paper towels
- scissors
- glue
- cotton wool balls, optional
- black felt pen
- thread
- tape

Art process
1. Stick the end of a branch in a coffee tin. Add sand around the branch so the ghost tree won't tip over. Cover the tin with coloured paper. Set this aside.
2. Draw a ghostly shape with glue on a heavy paper towel.
3. Press another paper towel to the first. You may choose to leave the bottom of the shape open to stuff and glue later. Dry the ghost.
4. Draw a face on the ghostly shape with the black pen.
5. Cut out the ghostly shape. If an opening was left at the bottom of the ghost, stuff the shape with cotton wool balls. Glue the end closed.
6. Tape a piece of thread to the ghost's head and hang the ghost from the tree branch.
7. Make more ghosts to hang from the branch until the sculpture is complete.

Variations
- Instead of ghosts make stuffed snowflakes, bears, hearts or geometric shapes. Experiment with papers of all types.
- Trace a hand on a doubled paper towel and make a ghost mitten or ghost puppet

Harvest art

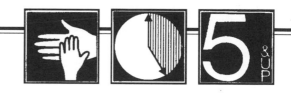

Materials

- leftover harvest foods in the field, orchard or garden such as corn husks, leaves, twigs, berries or nuts
- toothpicks, wooden matches, bamboo skewers, straight pins or string
- bits of paper, play clay, feathers or dried flowers
- permanent felt pens

Art process

1. Go for a walk in a field, orchard or garden and collect leftover harvest foods or other outdoor materials.
2. Create corn husk royalty, corn people, nut puppets, stick marionettes, feather birds, leaf masks or any other imaginative mobiles or designs.
3. Use string, skewers, toothpicks or other ideas to assemble the harvest art.
4. Add berries for eyes, bits of paper for capes and hats and pen marks for features. There really is no right or wrong way to create harvest art. The fun is being outside on a crisp day hunting for treasures from the earth to make things.
5. Take a few of the collected vegetables or fruits home to cook.
6. Bring the art home to enjoy or leave for wild creatures to discover and eat.

Variation

- Build little houses for the creatures from ferns, moss, sticks and holes dug into the earth. Add roads, worlds and more worlds.

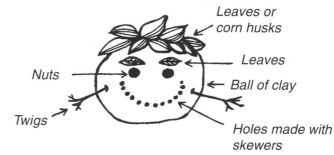

Leaves or corn husks

Leaves

Ball of clay

Holes made with skewers

Nuts

Twigs

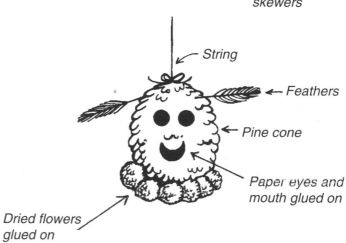

String

Feathers

Pine cone

Paper eyes and mouth glued on

Dried flowers glued on

HINT *Most of the harvest art creations will not hold together for robust play. Enjoy creating and playing on the day the art is made and prepare to bid them farewell fairly soon thereafter.*

Big spooky house

Materials
- large cardboard panel
- knife and scissors
- ready-mixed paint and paintbrushes
- paper and crayons
- masking tape

Art process
1. **Adult** helps cut the cardboard panel to look like a roof shape at the top. Under the direction of the artist, cut as many doors and windows as desired. Leave one side of the openings "hinged" so doors and windows will open and shut or cut a "capital I" shape so the openings open from the centre and fold back.
2. Place the panel flat on the floor and paint the house to have boards, bricks, shutters, roof tiles and other details. Dry completely.
3. Make spooky drawings on paper large enough to fit over the window and door openings. Draw ghosts, bats, pumpkins, trick-or-treaters and other Halloween images.
4. Tape the pictures over the openings from the back so the tape doesn't show.
5. Lean the spooky house panel up against a wall or door where it can be secured to stand on its own with tape or some other method.
6. Enjoy opening and closing the spooky doors and windows.

Variation
- Instead of a spooky Halloween theme, design a house, tree or vehicle with other types of characters inside. Some suggestions include forest creatures, storybook characters or aliens from another planet.

 HINT

Be prepared for some screams of delight.

Make smaller spooky houses with construction paper or smaller pieces of cardboard.

Peeky panel

Materials
- cardboard panel, about child-sized (cut from fridge or appliance box)
- knife and scissors
- white chalk
- ready-mixed paints
- large, flat paintbrushes
- small, fine paintbrushes
- large floor space for working

Art process
1. **Adult** helps trim the cardboard to chin-height of the artist. Next cut a semicircle into the top edge of the cardboard. Hand holes will be added later.
2. Place the cardboard flat on the floor. Using chalk, have the artist sketch a comical or realistic human form. Chalk can be rubbed off to change lines.
3. When the drawing is complete, an adult can cut the two circles for the hands or arms.
4. Next, place the cardboard flat again and paint the sketched body. Paint large areas first with a large flat brush. Let the paint dry. Use a small brush to paint the smaller more refined areas.
5. Add background in addition to details such as an umbrella in the hand or a dog on a lead. Dry the panel completely.
6. When dry, stand behind the panel, insert hands or arms through the two holes and rest the chin in the oval. Do this in front of a mirror or have a friend take a picture.

Variation
- With a small piece of cardboard, cut out a face shape. Design this panel with hair, a hat, ears, jewellery or other features. The artist may use this like a mask.

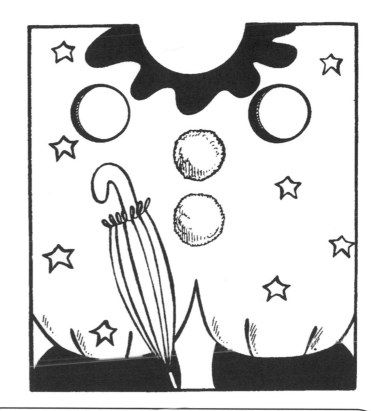

 Young artists enjoy the comical possibilities of this art form which also helps expand their awareness of the human form.

CONSTRUCTION

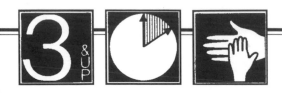

Crayon hands

Materials
- crayons
- pencils
- coloured paper and paper scraps
- scissors
- glue, tape, a stapler or paper fasteners

Art process
1. Use a crayon or pencil to trace the artist's hands on a piece of paper. Some artists prefer to trace their own hands without help.
2. Cut out the hand shapes. Trace and cut as many hand shapes as necessary for the chosen project. The design idea may be planned before the project is begun or evolve as the hands are traced.
3. Look over the hand shapes and try to think of something that could be made with the cut-outs. Some suggestions are a turkey, ghost, reindeer antlers, cat, chick, duck, bunny, angel wings, tulips, a butterfly or random hand designs.
4. Glue the hand shapes to paper and add other paper scraps or drawings to complete the design. Simply gluing hand shapes in an interesting design is enjoyable too.
5. Dry the completed project.

Variations
- Use tracing and cut-outs of bare feet for art ideas.
- Use paper fasteners for moving parts of the design.

HINT
Once young artists get the idea of seeing shapes in common objects, such as hands used for deer antlers, they will discover many shapes in all parts of their visual world.

D R A W I N G

Candle crayons

Materials
- candles (all shapes, sizes and colours)
- white paper
- watercolour paints and paintbrush
- cup of water
- crayons, optional
- covered work surface

Art process
1. Place a sheet of paper on the covered work surface.
2. Draw with candles of any size, shape and colour. Press hard for visible marks from many candles.
3. For an optional idea, draw and colour with crayon on the candle drawing.
4. To see the candle drawing, paint over the drawing with watercolour paint. This is called a wax-resist.
5. Dry the project completely. If drawing is very bubbled, wrinkled or curled, iron with a warm iron to flatten.

Variations
- Write secret messages with candles or draw pictures of a celebration on white lining paper covering a party table. Give each party guest a cup of coloured water and a paintbrush to uncover the secrets on the table.
- A wash of thinned ready-mixed paint or ink works as well as the watercolour paints.
- A dramatic wax-resist can be achieved by colouring very hard and brightly on paper with crayons and painting over the drawing with black or dark blue paint.

HINT *Rinse brush between colours in the plain water. Change water often for truest colours.*

Press hard with candles for a drawing that works with the watercolour paints.

DRAWING

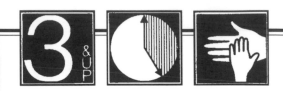

Fuzzy glue drawing

Materials
- scissors
- wool in contrasting colours to the background
- plastic bag or plastic container with lid for wool snips
- PVA glue in a dish (to colour white glue, mix glue with food colouring or ready-mixed paint)
- paintbrush for glue
- paper plate or board for the base
- covered work surface

Art process
1. Wind some wool about fifteen times around your fingers. Cut through the end of the loops.
2. Snip small pieces of the wool 1 cm or smaller into the plastic bag or container. (Cut different lengths or different colours if desired.)
3. Have the artist paint glue over a small area of the base.
4. The artist can choose a colour of wool and pat it down into the glued area.
5. Paint more glue in a different area and pat more wool into that glue. Continue making glue and wool designs or continue until the entire base is full.

Variation
- Cut different colours of wool and draw a picture with a glue bottle to create fuzzy wool pictures. Always work on small areas rather than large areas so glue won't dry out before the wool has been attached.

HINT
The one trick to a successful project is to spread the glue on to the base and press the wool into the glue. Do not dip the wool into the glue in the dish.

Adults can help with hand-wiping and wool-snipping but the artists should draw and cover the glue pictures.

Transparent crayon

Materials
- white paper
- crayons
- cooking oil
- cotton wool balls
- newspaper to cover table

Art process
1. Place white paper on the newspaper.
2. Draw freely with crayon on the white paper, pressing hard.
3. Rub a small amount of cooking oil over the back of the white paper using a cotton wool ball.
4. Dry the oil and crayon design on fresh newspaper.

Variations
- Use baby oil or mineral oil in place of cooking oil.
- Use a paintbrush to spread the oil instead of cotton wool balls.
- Experiment with different types of paper.

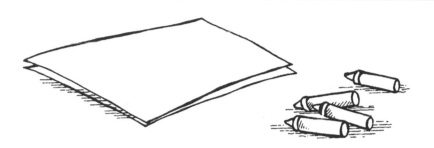

HINT — *Have a bucket of soapy warm water handy to wash oily hands.*

Some artists may not like the feeling or results of oil. Remember this is normal for young children.

Dot dots

Materials
- any drawing or colouring tools such as crayons, felt pens, paints and brushes, chalk, oil pastels or coloured pencils
- paper

Art process
1. Create an entire drawing or design using only dots of colour.
2. Change colours as desired.
3. Combine different art media such as using crayon dots for part of the design and paint dots for the background.

Variations
- Use contrasting colours such as green dots on red paper or yellow dots on purple paper.
- Pointillism is a technique of making paintings using nothing but dots to create a larger picture. This technique can easily be explored by young artists.

HINT *Look through a magnifying glass at colouring books in colour or comics and see how dots make up the entire picture. Young artists can usually understand the approach of dot dots drawing after looking through the magnifying glass or looking at the work of pointillist artists such as Seurat.*

Corn-cob print

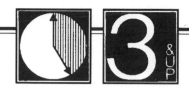

Materials
- dried corn-cobs without kernels
- ready-mixed paint on baking tray
- corn holders or nails
- large piece of paper
- covered work area

Art process
1. Save corn-cobs after sweetcorn has been eaten and dry them on a shelf.
2. Pour puddles of paint on a baking tray or tray.
3. Push corn holders into the ends of the corn-cob to use as handles while painting. If holders are not available, an **adult** can push nails into each end of the cob. If this doesn't work, just hold the ends of the cob with fingers.
4. Roll the corn-cob through the paint on the baking tray like a paint roller.
5. Roll the paint-covered cob across the large sheet of paper. Roll one long line or use back and forth movements. Make designs or any other shapes.
6. Dry the artwork.

Variation
- Use the corn-cob print for wrapping paper or backgrounds for other projects.

HINT *Sometimes this project works best on the floor so active artists can really roll the corn.*

Corn-cobs can be rinsed in water, dried and used again.

Negative space

Materials
- large sheets of newsprint
- scissors
- paint easel
- paints and brushes
- drying rack

Art process
1. With adult help cut a hole or shape out of the newsprint to be used for easel painting.
2. Attach the newsprint to the easel.
3. Paint on the paper using the negative space as part of the painting.
4. Remove the artwork from the easel and place on a drying rack.

Variations
- Cut paper into shapes for painting on the easel.
- Glue a coloured shape on the newsprint to incorporate in the painting.
- Use all of the negative space or shape ideas above with crayons or pens on paper.

HINT *Many artists are uncomfortable with a hole in the middle of their papers. Encourage them to enjoy the paper with the negative space.*

Fingerpaint monoprint

Materials
- scrap sugar paper
- scissors
- loop of masking tape
- fingerpaint (ready-mixed paint and liquid starch)
- baking tray or table top
- big piece of paper
- newspaper for drying paintings
- bucket of soapy water and towel for clean-up

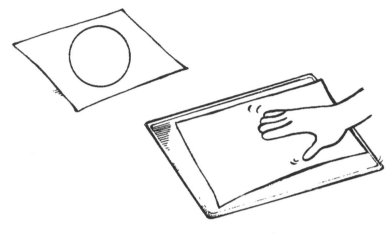

Art process
1. Cut a shape out of sugar paper such as a circle, a leaf, any design or shape.
2. Tape the shape to the centre of a sheet of paper with a loop of masking tape. Set the paper aside.
3. Pour a puddle of liquid starch in the middle of the baking tray. Place a spoonful of ready-mixed paint or powdered paint in the starch puddle.
4. Mix the starch and paint with the hands and continue fingerpainting on the baking tray. (If the paint is "resisting", add a few drops of liquid detergent to the fingerpaint.)
5. When the fingerpainting on the baking tray is complete, help the artist place the paper with the shape (shape side down) over the baking tray. Gently press and pat the paper to the fingerpainting design for a monoprint.
6. Peel the paper from the baking tray and place it on some newspaper to dry.
7. Gently peel or pull the paper shape from the painting; the unpainted shape will be surrounded by fingerpainting.

HINT *Have damp cloths handy for the artist to wipe fingers and hands.*

The drying area should be next to the printing area.

PAINTING

Twist and shout

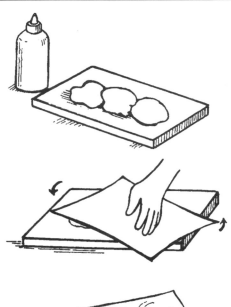

Materials
- squeezy bottles filled with ready-mixed paints
- heavy paper
- floor covered with newsprint
- large scrap of laminate from a counter top for paint surface
- sponges and soapy water for clean-up

Art process
1. Squeeze three to four big drops of paint directly on the scrap of counter top laminate on the floor.
2. Place a piece of heavy paper on the drops of paint.
3. Twist the paper with the heel of the palm about half a turn.
4. Lift and see the design.
5. Continue to experiment with colours and types of twisting to create new designs.
6. Sponge off the laminate with soapy water to make way for new creations or a change of artist.

Variations
- Make twisting designs with bare feet with or without paper.
- Use a paper plate or other types of paper for the twisting design.
- Use a table instead of the laminate from a counter top.
- Work on a baking tray instead of a table or laminate.

HINT

An adult should keep the laminate clean between artists or when a new creation is started. For this reason, this activity would work well outdoors where a bucket or hose could easily do the job.

Palette paint

Materials
- frozen dinner tray
- ready-mixed paints
- paintbrush
- jar of water and cloth
- paint easel
- paper

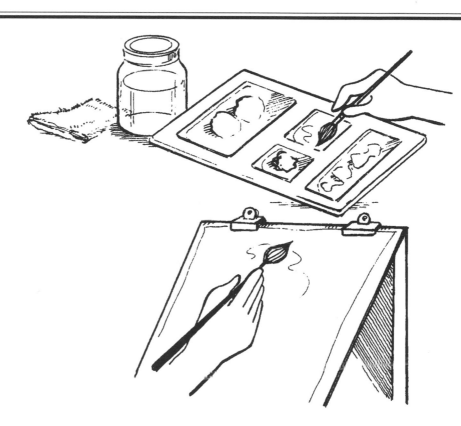

Art process
1. Place blobs of paint on a frozen dinner tray.
2. Have the artist stand at an easel holding the tray in one hand like a palette. Using one brush, mix shades and tints of paint on the palette to apply to the paper.
3. Rinse the brush in the water often. Use the cloth to dry the paintbrush as necessary.

Variations
- Use a pie plate or styrofoam lid instead of a frozen dinner plate for the palette. Use a real paint palette.
- Provide a palette knife (any plastic knife or craft stick will do) to experience dabbing and spreading paint on the easel.
- Some artists can experiment with acrylic paints.

HINT

Palette painting is an advanced step to be explored after a child has had some experience mixing paints in other art experiences. Young artists like to pretend they are famous adult artists standing at the easel and painting the way famous artists do. Provide a beret to add a dressing-up and pretend element to the activity.

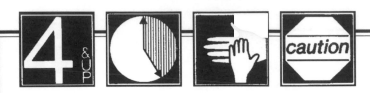

S
C
U
L
P
T
U
R
E

String thing

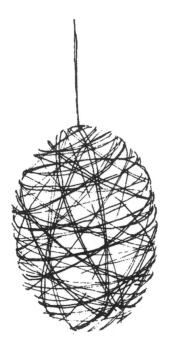

Materials
- granulated starch
- water
- pan
- stove
- cooker
- table covered with newspaper
- bowl
- colourful wool or embroidery threads (about 1 m long)
- a strong balloon

Art process
1. **Adult** makes the extra strong liquid starch. Dissolve one tablespoon of granulated starch in the amount of water stated on the starch package. Follow the rest of the instructions on the package. Place in a bowl and cool.
2. Blow up a balloon. Tie a double knot at the end.
3. Dip a string or piece of wool in the starch mixture. Make sure it is completely covered with starch but not too heavy to drape around the balloon.
4. Wrap the string around the balloon being sure to plaster down the ends of the string.
5. When the balloon is well covered with string (but not completely covered), dry the balloon overnight.
6. When the string is thoroughly dry, pop the balloon and remove it.
7. Use a piece of thread to hang the string thing from the ceiling, a branch or from some other framework.

HINT

The tendency to over-wrap the balloon is common. If too much string is used, it will just slip off the balloon in a pile on the table. Begin again and use less string.

Gently squeeze some of the starch out of the wool between two fingers and the wool will be sticky but not too heavy.

Stamped foil sculpture

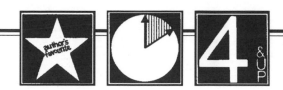

Materials
- aluminium foil, new or recycled
- masking tape
- board in black or other colour

Art process
1. Take a piece of foil and squeeze or bundle the piece into a ball or other shape.
2. Place the foil shape on the floor.
3. Stamp on it until it is completely flat.
4. Make small loops of masking tape and place them on the back of the flattened foil.
5. Press the flattened foil on the board until it sticks. Add more tape if necessary.

Variation
- Colour the board with chalk or paint for a colourful background for the stamped sculpture.
- Stamped foil sculptures can be suspended from the ceiling on black thread.

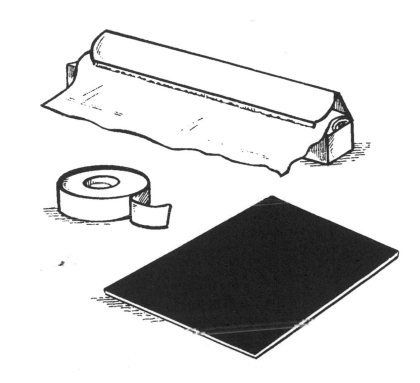

HINT

Stamped sculptures create interesting shapes and are an exhilarating art experience at any age.

Painted foil sculpture

Materials
- aluminium foil, recycled or new
- board or cardboard
- glue paint—mix tacky glue with ready-mixed paint and a few drops of liquid detergent
- glue gun, optional (to be used by an **adult**)
- paintbrush

Art process
1. Form one piece of foil into a shape or sculpture.
2. Mount the sculpture on board with tacky glue or glue paint. Allow plenty of time for the glue to dry. A quicker method is to have an **adult** use a glue gun and stick the foil shape to the board. Observe safety.
3. Paint the sculpture with glue paint. This allows the silver to shine through.
4. Dry the sculpture completely.

Variations
- Mix food colouring into the glue for a more transparent glue paint.
- Add more paint to the glue paint for an opaque glue paint.
- Combine wood scraps or other collage and sculpture materials to the foil sculpture.

HINT

Aluminum foil is a wonderful art medium and is inexpensive and convenient. Allow some experimentation and exploration for the artist. Recycle or reuse first attempts.

Detailed features, extensions or body parts are hard to accomplish with foil. Try to make the sculpture from one piece of foil.

Tray punch and sew

Materials
- styrofoam grocery tray
- tool for poking holes, such as pencil or scissors point
- pad of newspapers
- variety of pre-cut coloured wool, about 60 cm long
- masking tape

Art process
1. Place the styrofoam grocery tray on the pad of newspapers.
2. Poke holes, but not too many, with a pointed tool such as a pencil. (The artist may like to choose a number, such as ten, and poke only that many holes.)
3. Poke the holes in a random design or poke holes that suggest a picture or shape. More holes can always be poked later at any time during the project.
4. Wrap masking tape around the end of a piece of wool to resemble a needle and push through a hole in the tray.
5. Pull the wool all the way to the end of the yarn. Tape the end of the wool to the back of the grocery tray.
6. Continue sewing in and out of the holes to make a design. Change colours of wool at any time.
7. When the design is complete, tape the last end of wool to the back of the grocery tray.

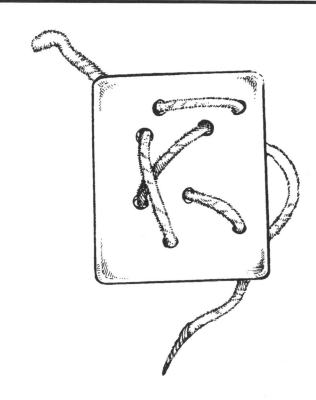

Variations
- Sew with yarn threaded on a large plastic needle.
- Do not pre-poke holes in the styrofoam tray. Sew on the grocery tray with yarn threaded on a plastic needle and poke holes as in embroidery.

HINT *Sometimes artists need help threading a needle, taping the end of the wool for a needle and untangling knots and loops that sometimes form.*

CRAFT

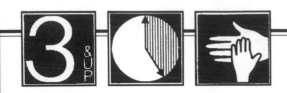

Masterpiece collection

Materials
- children's artwork
- glue and tape
- scrapbook with blank pages
- felt pen

Art process
1. To save favourite artwork in a scrapbook, choose a piece of art and glue or tape it into the scrapbook. The book can be organized in specific sections or randomly as the year progresses.
2. An adult may write down the artist's comments about specific artwork placed in the scrapbook. Do not write on the artwork. Some questions to ask the artists include: "What did you like about this artwork", "Tell me about your masterpiece" or "Tell me about the colours you chose."
3. Continue to save flat artwork in the scrapbook until it is full.

Variations
- Some artists prefer a scrapbook where they create directly on each scrapbook page.
- Make a homemade scrapbook. Stack large sheets of paper together. Punch holes on one side of the paper. Punch holes in a cardboard cover. String the scrapbook together with wool and begin saving artwork or photographs in this homemade scrapbook.

HINT *The artist should choose what to save for the collection.*

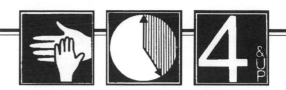

Cuff finger puppets

Materials
- old pair of trousers with deep cuffs or hem
- sewing machine
- scissors
- materials for decorating the puppets including sewing scraps, wool, buttons, plastic eyes or felt
- tacky glue or needle and thread

Art process
1. Turn an old pair of trousers with deep cuffs inside out. Cut straight across the hem.
2. With adult help sew two "U" shapes on each cuff so that the hem of the cuff will be the bottom of each finger puppet. Cut 8 mm from the edge of the sewn line. Turn the cuff right-side out or leave as it is.
3. Decorate the cuff puppets with any variety of sewing or craft items using glue or a needle and thread. Puppets can be animals, people, characters from a book or story or strange little shapes with no real adult understanding.
4. Make up plays, songs or simply enjoy the puppets.

Variation
- Decorate a box for storing a growing collection of cuff puppets. Develop a group of puppets that can be stored together such as the three cuff bears and one golden-haired cuff girl.

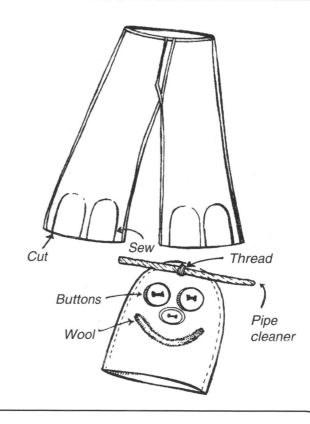

 HINT *Each pair of trousers makes approximately four cuff puppets.*

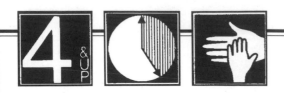

C R A F T

Easy store puppet stage

Materials
- one spring-tension curtain rod to fit a doorway
- old sheet
- fabric pens
- glue paints (tacky glue and ready-mixed paint mixed together)
- dishes for paints
- paintbrushes
- sewing machine, optional

Art process
1. Spread a spring-tension curtain rod in a doorway at a height suitable for young puppeteers.
2. With fabric pens or glue paint, decorate an old sheet for the puppet curtain. Dry the curtain completely.
3. Drape the sheet over the rod and produce a puppet show by crouching behind the curtain.
4. As an optional idea, sew a simple casing at the top of a decorated sheet cut to fit the doorway and rod. Push the curtain rod through the casing and place it in the doorway.
5. To store the puppet stage, roll the curtain up around the rod and put it in any corner or spare cupboard space.

Variation
- Make a glamorous curtain by adding glitter to the wet glue paint.

HINT

Remember that sometimes puppeteers need help winding up a long production with a gentle hint that the show will end in a few more minutes.

Circle weave

Materials
- board or cardboard cut into circles, any size
- scissors
- wool, many colours cut about 60 cm long
- masking tape

Art process
1. With adult help cut cardboard or board into circles of any size. (About 10 cm across is a manageable size for young hands.)
2. Help the artist cut about five or six slits around the edge of each circle with scissors.
3. Weave the circle shape by winding wool around and around the circle taking the wool through one of the slits with each pass. Experiment with criss-cross designs.
4. Tape or tie the end of the wool on the back of the circle. Bend in the edges between the slits, if desired.

Variation
- Cut other shapes from matte board or cardboard such as a tree, square or heart.
- Use embroidery thread in place of wool.

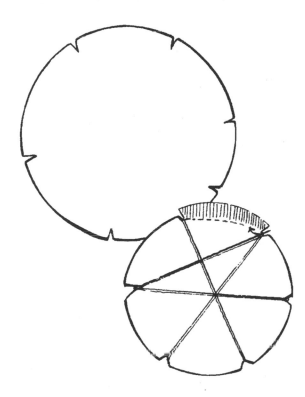

HINT For an easy wool dispenser, place a ball of wool in a margarine tub. Cut a hole in the lid of the tub. Pull the wool end through the hole and then snap on the lid. The wool will unwind without tangling.

Scrimshaw pendant

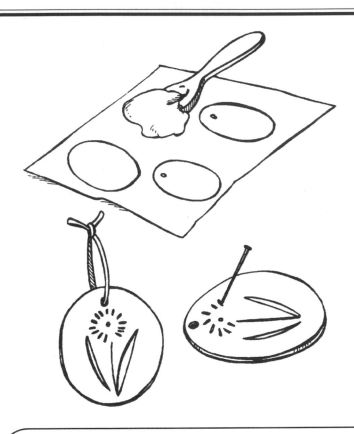

Materials
- 70 g plaster of Paris
- 150 ml water
- nail or pin
- felt pens
- measuring jug
- leather thong
- spoon
- varnish, optional
- greaseproof paper
- cloth

Art process
1. Mix 70 g plaster of Paris into 150 ml of water in a measuring jug with a spoon until thick and smooth. Remember to work fast because plaster hardens quickly.
2. Drop spoonfuls of plaster on the greaseproof paper. Harden for five to ten minutes. If necessary, smooth plaster with the back of a spoon.
3. If a necklace is planned, poke a hole in the top of the plaster blob on the wax paper while the plaster is still soft.
4. Scratch a design in the plaster with a nail or pin to etch a design just like the whalers did on shark tooth, whale bone and walrus tusk.
5. Draw on the scratched design with felt pens and then rub away the excess. The ink will fill the scratches.
6. Draw additional designs and pictures on the plaster, if desired.
7. Cover the pendant with varnish, if desired, to preserve the design.
8. Run a leather thong through the hole and wear the plaster scrimshaw as a pendant or necklace.

HINT
Young artists sometimes make very large pendants—very large—but enjoy wearing them anyway.

Cinnamon drawing

Materials
- cinnamon sticks
- sandpaper
- scissors

Art process
1. Cut the sandpaper into shapes or use as it is.
2. Draw on the sandpaper with a cinnamon stick.

Variations
- Cut the sandpaper into holiday shapes and string on wood with other decorations between each shape. You can use styrofoam peanuts, pieces of foil, pieces of coloured paper or wrapping paper, playdough beads or other interesting items. Hang the garland from the ceiling around the room. Mmmmm, it smells nice too!
- Cut little squares of sandpaper and string a necklace on wool. Punch holes with a paper punch in the small cinnamon squares of sandpaper. This make a nice smelling necklace.
- Glue glitter or wool to the edge of the sandpaper designs to decorate.

HINT

Sandpaper is difficult to cut and can blunt scissors.

Young artists like to really scribble and scrub the cinnamon on the sandpaper for the fragrance more than the design.

Fabric transfer

Materials
- fabric crayons
- white paper
- fabric—old sheet, muslin, a T-shirt or pillowcase
- old iron
- pad of newspaper for ironing

Art process
1. Draw or colour heavily with fabric crayons on white paper (follow the directions on the fabric crayon box).
2. Place the fabric on the pad of newspaper.
3. Place the drawing face down on the fabric.
4. **Adult** presses the paper with a warm iron using a firm, straight ironing motion. The picture from the fabric crayons will transfer to the fabric.
5. Remove the piece of paper with the fabric crayon design. The wax will have melted into the fabric and the heat will set the colour into the fabric.

Variations
- Individual squares could be sewn into a quilt.
- Decorate a bandana, book bag, cloth napkins, table cloth or any other fabric idea.

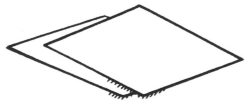

HINT

Fabric crayons are available from fabric and craft shops and often in art supply areas of shops that carry ordinary crayons.

Drawings made from fabric crayon will not look like drawings made with ordinary crayons but the transferred design will have bright and true colours. The colours may look different from ordinary crayons.

As with any ironing project, an adult should either do the ironing or supervise older artists with the ironing.

DRAWING

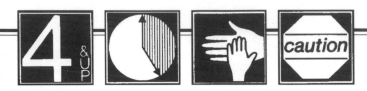

Stained glass melt

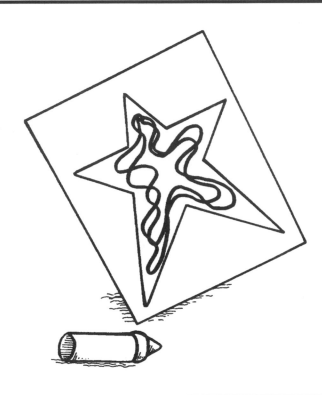

Materials
- white paper
- black felt pens
- old crayons, peeled
- warming tray
- heavy glove or oven glove
- scissors and tape, optional

Art process
1. Use the black felt pen to outline a design on the white paper. The blank spaces will be "coloured in" with melted crayon.
2. Place the paper with black outline drawing on the warming tray.
3. Put a heavy glove or oven glove on the non-drawing hand. Hold the paper down with this hand.
4. Using the peeled crayons, colour in the pen design. Working slowly will allow the crayon to melt and soak into the paper.
5. Remove the design from the warming tray. Hold the paper up to the light or a window and see the stained glass effect.
6. The design can be cut out and displayed in a window to resemble a stained glass window.

Variations
- Artists can observe real stained glass windows which will enhance their imaginations as they create.
- Rub the back of the crayon design with a cotton wool ball soaked in baby oil for a more transparent design.

HINT

As with any project involving heat or electricity, observe safety and caution. Tape the cord from the warming tray to the table and push the table against the wall.

Some young artists will not have the concept of stained glass and will simply enjoy melting crayon in pretty but random patterns.

Peeled glue

Materials
- bottle of PVA glue
- greaseproof paper
- felt pens
- thread or wool
- newspaper to cover table

Art process
1. Drip glue on a piece of greaseproof paper in a design. Make thick masses, shapes or forms.
2. Dry the glue until hard and clear.
3. Decorate the dry glue shapes with felt pens.
4. Carefully peel the dry, decorated glue shapes off the wax paper.
5. The shapes can be laced with thread or wool and hung from the ceiling, worn as jewellery or used as festive decorations.

Variations
- Mix ready-mixed paint into the glue for a coloured glue.
- Sprinkle glitter or salt on the glue before it dries for a sparkling effect.

D R A W I N G

HINT

Peeling the glue takes some patience and coordination so an adult may wish to help with this step.

It may take several days until the glue dries clear and hard, depending on weather conditions.

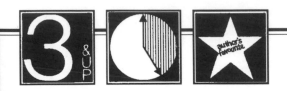

Paper drop dye

Materials
- variety of papers—rice paper, coffee filter, blotting paper or paper towels
- food colouring in several bowls
- eyedroppers
- newsprint to cover table
- old shirt or smock

Art process
1. Cover the table with newsprint.
2. Place a piece of absorbent paper on the newsprint.
3. Fill an eyedropper with colour from one bowl and drop a spot of colour on to the paper.
4. Use another eyedropper to add another colour. The colours will blend to make a pattern.
5. Transfer the paper to a clean piece of newsprint to dry.

Variations
- When the project is dry, paper can be cut into a snowflake design, used as wrapping paper or hung in a window to enjoy the bright colours.
- Fold and dip the paper into the bowls or colour instead of using the eyedroppers.
- Use powdered paint or fabric dye available from art shops instead of food colouring. Although these dyes seem expensive, they last a long time, go a long way and come in an amazing rainbow of bright colours.

HINT

Many young artists become absorbed in the blending of colours and end up with a substantially soaked piece of paper which can be difficult to move. Work on a sheet of newsprint sturdy enough to hold the finished artwork that can be lifted and carried to a drying location.

Expect fingers and hands to be stained. The colour can take several days to wash out. Protect clothing with an old shirt or smock.

Shiny painting

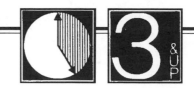

Materials
- paint mixture: ready-mixed paint for colour, 4 tablespoons golden syrup, 1 1/2 teaspoons washing-up liquid
- board or cardboard
- paintbrushes
- mixing spoons
- small containers

Art process
1. Make the paint mixture of ready-mixed paint, syrup and washing-up liquid. Place the paint in small containers.
2. Paint freely with the mixture using any painting approach on board or cardboard for a sturdy base.

Variations
- Dip string or wool into the shiny paint and press between sheets of paper for a shiny wool design. Then remove wool.
- Place paper in a baking pan and roll marbles through puddles of shiny paint.
- Use the shiny paint on white or coloured tissue paper to create wrapping paper.

 HINT
This paint is very pretty and glossy which makes it nice for festive themes.

This paint is also very sticky and dries more slowly than ordinary paint.

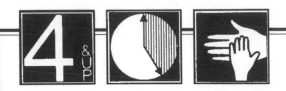

Insole stamps

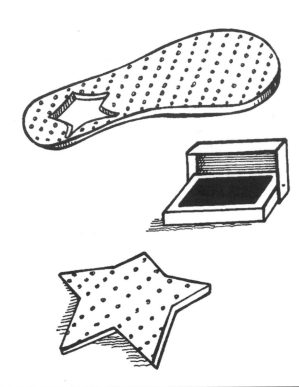

Materials
- shoe insoles
- pen
- scissors
- rubber cement
- wooden block scrap
- ink pad or paint spread on paper towels

Art process
1. Draw a design on the latex side (not the fabric side) of the insole.
2. Cut out the design with scissors.
3. Glue the cut-out shape to a scrap of wood with rubber cement.
4. When dry, press the block stamp into an ordinary ink pad. (If no ink pads are available, spread some paint or food colouring on a pad of paper towels in a styrofoam tray and use like an ink pad.)

Variations
- The insole shape can be glued to a jar lid or a piece of heavy cardboard.
- Use this idea for decorating festive wrapping paper or making greetings cards.

HINT

Some young children tend of think that the harder they smash the stamp into the ink, the better the print will be. Encourage gentle but firm pressing for the best print ever.

Other glues will also work if rubber cement is not available or objectionable due to the odour or fumes it emits.

Stained glass painting

Materials
- white drawing paper
- permanent black marking pen
- bright ready-mixed paints in cups
- paintbrushes

Art process
1. Draw bold black lines on the paper using the marking pen.
2. Paint inside the lines with bright ready-mixed paints.

Variations
- For a shiny paint, see "Shiny painting" (page 119) for this project.
- Paint black lines with black paint. When dry, fill in the black line with bright paints.

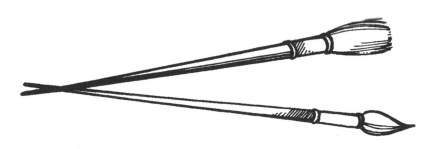

HINT

Permanent pens soak through paper and can stain the table so cover the table with plastic or newsprint. Any marks on the table can be removed with powdered cleanser. To remove pen marks from clothes, spray the stain with hairspray, rinse, spray again and rinse again. Continue this pattern until the stain is completely gone.

Some people prefer not to use permanent pens with young children due to the fumes from the ink. The decision is yours.

PAINTING

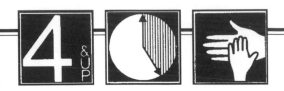

Snow paint

Materials
- dark sugar paper such as purple and blue
- crayons
- paintbrushes
- 4 tablespoons Epsom salts
- 60 ml hot water
- small cups or bowls
- spoons
- covered table

Art process
1. Mix 60 ml hot water with 4 tablespoons of Epsom salts. Stir the mixture to dissolve.
2. Draw freely with the crayons on the dark sugar paper.
3. Brush the drawing with the salt mixture.
4. Dry the painting completely.

Variation
- Cut snowy designs from the paper and hang them with string.

 HINT

The salt will dry to a snowy, crystal effect.

Stir the salt water each time a brush is dipped into the container to keep the brush full of very salty water.

Table salt or rock salt can be substituted for Epsom salts.

Window painting

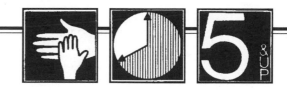

Materials
- paintbrushes
- newspaper
- tape
- ready-mixed paints in containers

Art process
1. Tape newspaper to the bottom edges of the windows to protect floors and ledges.
2. Paint the inside of the window so rain will not wash off the painting.
3. Leave the design on the windows for days or weeks.
4. Wash the design off with a sponge and soapy water. (This is a messy job!)

Variations
- Paint festive scenes or designs or use festive colours to paint any designs.
- Cover the window with a large sheet of cellophane and paint on the cellophane instead of the window.
- Paint with white shoe polish and the applicators which come in the polish bottles. This is very easy to clean up. White is nice for snow scenes, too.

 HINT

Mix powdered paint with washing-up liquid and water for easier removal.

Mix paint with white shoe polish for optional easy removal.

The longer the paint is left on the window, the harder it is to remove.

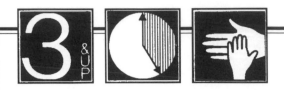

Sugar mint modelling

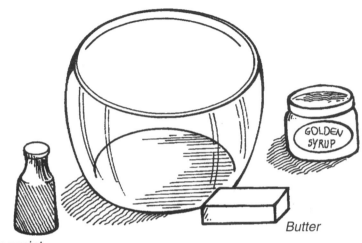

Peppermint extract

Butter

Materials
- dough mixture:
    - 70 g butter or margerine
    - 75 ml golden syrup
    - 1 teaspoon peppermint extract
    - 1/2 teaspoon salt
    - 450 g icing sugar
- food colouring
- large bowl
- small bowls
- spoon

Art process
1. Be sure hands are clean before beginning this activity.
2. Mix all the ingredients except the food colouring in a large bowl.
3. Divide the mixture into separate small bowls, one for each colour desired.
4. With a spoon, stir drops of food colouring into each bowl.
5. With clean hands, create designs and sculptures with the sugar mint mixture. Combine and mix colours too.
6. Sugar mint sculptures are edible but are very, very sweet.

Variation
- Experiment with other flavourings such as almond, vanilla or lemon instead of mint.

HINT *Fingers and faces get sticky (surprise!) so have warm water and towels available. Also, warm little hands can soften the dough substantially; this is when things start to get sticky.*

Sculptures can be refrigerated. They will harden somewhat. Give the finished sculptures as gifts wrapped in cellophane or cling film and tied with a bow. Artists may want to eat their creation right on the spot.

Bread sculpture

D O U G H

Materials
- 1 tablespoon dry yeast
- 230 ml water
- 1 teaspoon sugar
- 400 g flour
- 1 tablespoon oil
- 400ºF (200 ºC) oven
- cooling rack
- kitchen tools for modelling (knife, fork, toothpick)

- 1 teaspoon salt
- mixing bowl
- wooden spoon
- clean towel

Art process
1. Wash hands before beginning. Mix the water, sugar and yeast in a bowl until the yeast softens (about two to three minutes).
2. Add 200 g of flour and stir vigorously with a wooden spoon. Beat the mixture until smooth and add one tablespoon of oil and one teaspoon of salt. Next add the remaining 200 g of flour to the dough.
3. Pour the thick batter on to a floured board and add more flour slowly while kneading the dough. Keep a coating of flour on the dough to prevent sticking.
4. Knead for about five minutes. The dough should be smooth, elastic and satiny and should bounce back if a finger is poked into it. Place the dough in an oiled bowl and cover with a clean towel. Set the bowl in a warm place and allow the dough to rise for about forty-five minutes.
5. Punch the dough down and work it into a smooth ball. Divide the dough into portions for various parts of the bread sculpture or for different children to use.

6. Create sculptures with the dough. Create any shapes or designs.
7. Bake the sculptures for fifteen to twenty minutes in the lower part of a 400ºF (200 ºC) oven. Large forms may take longer. Bake until golden and baked through. Cool the sculptures on a rack. Eat and enjoy.

 HINT *Bread dough sculptures work well for Christmas and other holidays.*

Young artists like to keep a small bowl of flour handy to keep their hands powdery while working. Sometimes they like the soft flour better than the sculptures.

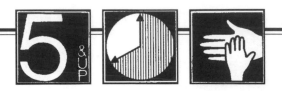

Marzipan fantasy fruits

DOUGH

Materials
- marzipan
- food colouring
- cloves
- sliced almonds
- clean work surface
- airtight containers or cling film

Art process
1. Wash hands before beginning. Break marzipan into several balls, one ball for each colour of fantasy fruit.
2. Add a little food colouring to each ball and work the colouring into the marzipan with hands.
3. Using the coloured marzipan, create real fruits, imaginary fruits or any shapes and designs.
4. Add sliced almonds for leaves and cloves for stems to the designs.
5. Store marzipan fruits in airtight containers or with cling film. The fruits are edible.

Variations
- Make sculptures other than fruits such as balloons, clowns, animals, flowers or abstract shapes.
- Use this project as gifts for the holidays.

Royal icing art

Materials

- 250 g icing sugar
- 1 egg white at room temperature (or powdered egg whites)
- 1/2 teaspoon lemon juice
- egg beater or electric mixer
- small bowl
- tasty decorations including chocolates, biscuits, sweets, marshmallows, sprinkles or shredded coconut
- pipe cleaners
- spreading knives
- foil-covered cardboard or a pizza cardboard circle

Art process

1. An adult should beat the egg white until stiff.
2. Add sifted icing sugar a tablespoon at a time, beating after each addition.
3. When the icing is a thick spreading consistency, add the lemon juice which helps with quick drying.
4. Work on the foil covered cardboard or pizza circle. Use the icing as cement or glue and stick biscuits together to make animals, toys or festive scenes.
5. Eat right away or display for all to see and enjoy.

Variation

- Make little biscuit houses; a barnyard scene with a marshmallow pig and bread stick fence; a Santa face with white icing beard and jelly bean nose; a ski scene with toy skiers on icing hills or other creative ideas.

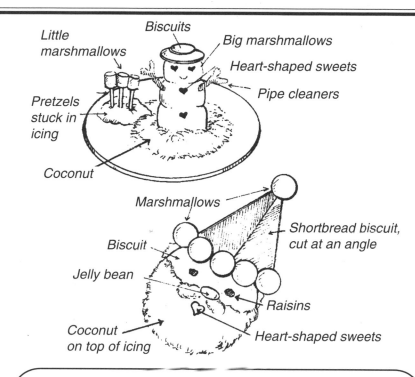

Little marshmallows

Biscuits

Big marshmallows

Heart-shaped sweets

Pipe cleaners

Pretzels stuck in icing

Coconut

Marshmallows

Biscuit

Jelly bean

Shortbread biscuit, cut at an angle

Raisins

Coconut on top of icing

Heart-shaped sweets

HINT

As with any edible activity, wash hands before beginning.

Royal icing can be doubled, tripled or made in any quantity. However, for large batches, keep a damp cloth over the bowl to prevent the icing from drying out. Excess icing can be stored in airtight containers in the fridge for up to a week.

Using powdered egg whites will avoid the risk of salmonella poisoning.

Sweet insects

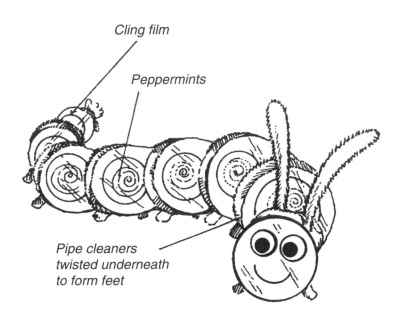

Cling film

Peppermints

Pipe cleaners
twisted underneath
to form feet

Materials
- cling film
- coloured pipe cleaners
- ribbons, rubber bands and string
- small sweets
- dried fruits such as apricots
- toothpicks

Art process
1. Place sweets on a strip of cling film and wind the cling film around them to form a caterpillar or other insect shapes.
2. Twist pipe cleaners between sweets or at appropriate intervals to form the head, body and legs. Use rubber bands, string or ribbons too.
3. Sweet insects make delicious treats or great party bag fillers for birthdays.

Variation
- Toothpicks can be stuck into the insect for spines, antennae, stingers or teeth.

HINT *Any time you are working with something as tempting as sweets, it is a good idea to have some available for eating.*

Hands can get sticky, so have a washing bucket ready. Always begin with clean hands when working with food.

Cling film can be difficult to control so keep pieces small or help the young artist with the wrapping.

String ornaments

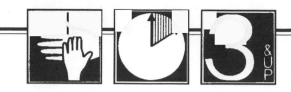

Materials
- various lengths of string or embroidery thread
- PVA glue, thinned with water in a small bowl
- greaseproof paper
- glitter
- scissors
- wet towel for clean-up

Art process
1. Dip the string in the thinned glue.
2. Wipe excess glue off the string by pulling it through the index finger and thumb or by pulling it across the edge of the bowl.
3. Place the string on the greaseproof paper in any shape, design, pattern or form.
4. Sprinkle glitter over the string.
5. Dry the string design completely.
6. Gently peel the string design off the greaseproof paper.
7. Hang the string as an ornament if desired.

Variations
- Make definite shapes such as circles, stars, diamonds or other designs with the string.
- Add ready-mixed paint to the thinned glue for a coloured glue.
- Sprinkle other things on the ornaments such as coloured sand, confetti or cake sprinkles.

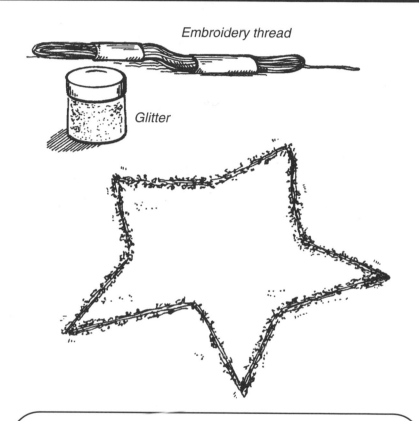

Embroidery thread

Glitter

HINT

This project will need to dry at least overnight.

Peeling the string from the greaseproof paper can be tricky.

C
R
A
F
T

Tile marking

Materials
- white ceramic tiles
- permanent felt markers
- apron

Art process
1. Draw on white ceramic tiles with permanent markers.
2. Tiles dry quickly.

Variations
- Use decorated tiles for trivets or mats to protect the table from hot dishes or foods.
- Tiles make nice gifts.
- Decorate the tiles with holiday themes for holiday gifts or decorations.

HINT   Free tiles can be collected from contractors who have leftover tiles, or contact a local DIY store for tile samples or leftovers.

Pens can stain so prepare by covering the table, child or anything in the work area which could possibly be damaged.

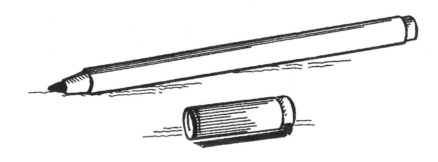

Light holes

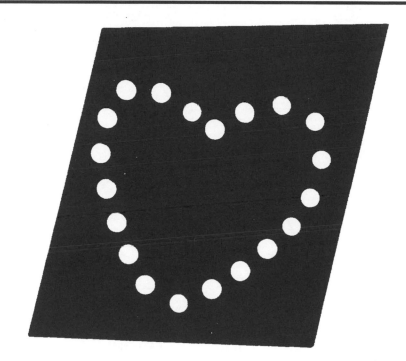

**C
R
A
F
T**

Materials
- black paper
- heavy cardboard for work surface
- poking tools such as a pencil, nail, pin, bamboo skewer or scissors
- tape
- glue
- scraps of coloured tissues, cellophane and coloured paper

Art process
1. Tape a square of black paper to the cardboard work surface.
2. Use the poking tools to punch holes in the black paper. Make as many hole in as many sizes as desired.
3. Remove the tape.
4. Cover the holes with any coloured paper by gluing or taping the papers on the back of the black paper. It is pretty to cover each hole or few holes with small scraps of tissue or cellophane.
5. Place the design in a window or hold it up to the light to see the coloured lights.

Variations
- Make holes in a pattern or design.
- Work on black paper that has been cut into a pattern such as a tree, star or circle.
- Poke holes in coloured paper and tape the paper to a sheet of black paper. The holes seem to "pop out" using this method.
- Glue the poked paper on a sheet of foil for shiny holes.
- Use a piece of plywood for the work surface and make all the holes using a hammer and nails.

HINT

When working with sharp tools supervise closely. Allow plenty of room between artists and set a rule that all sharp objects must be left on the table if the artist must get up for any reason.

Some artists have not learned to control poking holes through paper. The paper can tear rather than making a hole. Paper tears can be taped on the back or may be incorporated into the design.

Photo sculpture

Magazine picture

Polystyrene board

Frame scraps

HINT

Sometimes the glue leaks down between the wood scraps and the photo sculpture ends up stuck to the table. To prevent this from happening, move the sculptures often or dry them on a baker's cooling rack or wire mesh screen. Lift the sculptures when dry.

The photo sculpture has a life-like look when displayed.

Materials
- magazine picture or photograph
- polystyrene board (from an art shop or school supply catalogue)
- PVA glue (thinned with water in a dish) or rubber cement (as is)
- brush for glue
- scissors
- 2 picture frame scraps, equal lengths
- tape or rubber bands
- glue gun, optional

Art process
1. Carefully cut out a good-sized photograph or magazine picture for the sculpture.
2. Place the picture on a polystyrene board and trace the outline. Remove the picture. **Adult** cuts the polystyrene on the traced line.
3. Glue the picture to the polystyrene being careful to stick the edges down and smooth out the wrinkles.
4. Dry the picture completely.
5. Trim any excess picture or polystyrene if necessary.
6. For the base, put glue on the inside edges of two frame scraps. Place the photo sculpture upright between the frame pieces and press them together with the photograph between them. Hold the frames together using tape or rubber bands until dry.
7. For the magazine picture sculptures, paint a coat of PVA glue over the entire sculpture including the frame scrap base and all the edge of the polystyrene.

C R A F T

Advent boxes

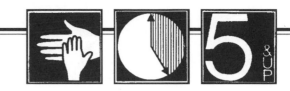

Materials
- 24 small boxes (jewellery or match boxes)
- Christmas wrapping paper scraps
- ribbon
- tape
- sweets, nuts or small toys
- 24 labels
- pen
- scissors

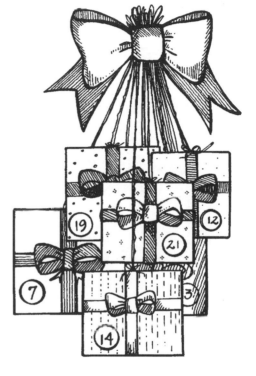

Art process
1. Fill each box with sweets, nuts or small toys.
2. Wrap each box with wrapping paper scraps.
3. Tie each box with ribbon. Curl ends of ribbon if desired.
4. Label each box with numbers from one to twenty-four.
5. Cut twenty-four long pieces of ribbon and tie one to each box.
6. Adjust the way the boxes hang so they hang at different lengths.
7. Gather all the ribbons in one hand at the top, divide them into two bunches and tie the two bunches together in a knot or bow. Add an even larger bow to the top of the advent box hanging, if desired.
8. Hang up the advent boxes and open one box each day, starting on the first of December. The twenty-fourth box will be opened on Christmas Eve.

Variation
- Other ideas for things to put in each box include: wishes for others, little drawings or pictures of holiday things, or greetings from Christmas cards.

HINT *Most of this activity is adult-assisted. The fun for the child is opening the boxes each day. Wrapping the boxes is something children can do, but keep in mind that they don't do it the way adults would.*

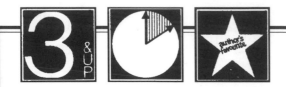

D R A W I N G

Chalk dip

Materials
- coloured chalk
- 1 tablespoon thick, white ready-mixed paint
- jar lid
- black or dark paper

Art process
1. Dip the end of a piece of coloured chalk into some thick white ready-mixed paint in a jar lid.
2. Draw with the whitened, moist chalk. The marks will show the distinct colour of the chalk edged with white paint against the dark paper.

Variations
- Make a sampler of markings such as zigzags, spirals, curves, straight lines and other markings on dark paper.
- Experiment with dipping the chalk with black paint and then working on white paper.

HINT

Scrubbing with the paint-dipped chalk creates a mixed, blurry tint instead of the colour edged in white.

Chalk can blur and smudge on hands, clothes and on the paper. This is a natural occurrence when young children work with chalk.

Glue and chalk draw

Materials
- PVA glue in squeezy bottle
- coloured chalk
- dark paper
- hairspray as a fixative, optional

Art process
1. Draw a freeform design on dark paper with glue.
2. Dry the glue overnight.
3. Apply coloured chalk to the areas between the clear glue lines. The glue lines will appear to be black and the chalk will have a muted effect on the other area.
4. An **adult** can spray the chalk and glue drawing with a fixative if desired. Hairspray works well. Spray the artwork outside or in a well-ventilated area away from the children.

Variations
- Draw with glue on white paper, dry and then paint the spaces between the glue lines. The lines will appear white.
- An adult can add black India ink to the glue. Follow the same steps on white or black paper, using watercolours or chalk to fill in the spaces.

HINT

The black paper dulls the chalk so it has a muted effect.

Chalk is always messy for young artists; this is to be expected and enjoyed. Have warm, soapy water handy for clean-up.

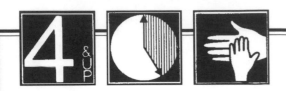

DRAWING

Little art books

Materials
- light scrap paper or newsprint (cut into 3 or 4 strips about 6 cm x 20 cm)
- heavy paper for the book cover (6 cm x 20 cm)
- stapler, hole punch and wool, paper fasteners, or pipe cleaners for binding
- crayons or markers

Art process
1. **Adult** folds three to four strips of scrap paper in half.
2. **Adult** adds a cover to the strips. Staple the entire booklet together or use some other form of binding. The booklet can be put together using a hole punch and wool, paper fasteners or pipe cleaners.
3. The artist can draw pictures or designs on each page.
4. Decorate the cover.

Variations
- Use index cards stapled together.
- Make little art books with different colours of paper and set out different types of drawing materials such as coloured pencils, stencils, a ruler and tape.

HINT

Young artists can make their own books after they have been shown how. Staplers are fascinating to young artists so be prepared for a substantially stapled creation.

If the artist has a title for the book, offer to write it on the front along with any other writing or dictation the artist might like on each page too.

Zigzag gallery

Materials
- 2 A4 pieces of cardboard for the cover
- board or posterboard cut into A4 pieces for the pages
- masking tape or cloth library tape
- crayons, pens

Art process
1. Draw a series of pictures or designs which tell a story. Pictures may also be a collection of thoughts or designs based on one theme or topic. You may also use a collection of favourite drawings.
2. An **adult** should tape the boards together with masking tape or cloth library tape so that the pages fold in an accordion style.
3. Add the cardboard cover with tapes.
4. Fold the zigzag book into a book shape or display the opened gallery on a table or shelf.

Variations
- Cut out shapes from paper or wallpaper scraps and paste the shapes on each board instead of drawing.
- Illustrate a favourite story or fairy tale.
- Make a zigzag book that has no sequence or collection of thoughts but is simply a collection of artwork, drawings and designs.

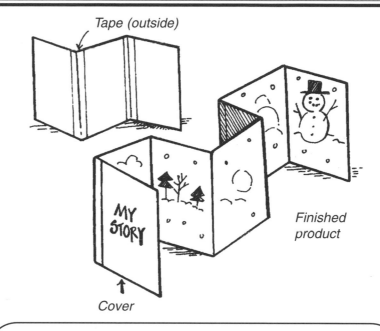

Tape (outside)

Finished product

Cover

HINT

The taping of the pages together is definitely an adult step.

Sequence can be a bit abstract for very young artists, but this project can help make sense of it.

Cutting the boards in a square, eg 25 x 25 cm, eliminates the problem of a drawing being sideways in the finished product.

Library fabric tape comes in many colours from school supply catalogues and works well in place of masking tape.

Snowy etching

Materials
- crayons
- white drawing paper, any size
- scraping tool such as blunt pencil, scissors point, paper-clip or spoon

Art process
1. Using muscles and determination, completely colour a piece (or a section) of white drawing paper. Colour hard and shiny using various colours of blue, white and grey crayons.
2. Using black or dark blue, colour over the first layer of colours.
3. When complete, scratch a design of a snowman, a snowy day, snowflakes or any other design into the top layer of crayon. The first layer will show through.

Variations
- Instead of a second layer of crayon, use white or black paint over the first layer of crayon. Then finger paint in the paint. The slick, shiny crayon background will act like finger painting paper.
- Colour a square, circle or other shape in the centre of the paper, reducing the challenge of colouring such a large area.

HINT

Smooth board instead of paper works very well in this project. Paper can sometimes wrinkle and tear with vigorous colouring.

Recommended for artists with enough patience and muscular strength to colour a thick layer over a fulll sheet of paper. Not all artists should be expected to work at this pace or intensity.

Five block prints

Materials
- 5 printing materials: 1. insulation tape (peel-off variety); 2. styrofoam grocery tray; 3. felt scraps; 4. cardboard strips; and 5. string
- 5 wooden blocks
- PVA glue in squeezy bottle
- scissors
- ready-mixed paint
- old flannel
- water
- baking tray
- paper

Art process
1. Cut each of the five printing materials into shapes or patterns and glue each one to a block of wood. (The insulation tape will stick on its own.) Allow the glue to dry.
2. Meanwhile, dampen an old flannel in water and wring it out.
3. Place it on a baking tray.
4. Spread ready-mixed paint on the damp flannel to be used as the stamp pad.
5. Press a dry woodblock design into the paint and then press it on to the paper.
6. Combine different print designs or make patterns using only one block per piece of paper

Variations
- Use food colouring, paste food colouring, dye, inks or ink pads for the printing step instead of paint.
- Make wrapping paper by printing on large sheets of white tissue.

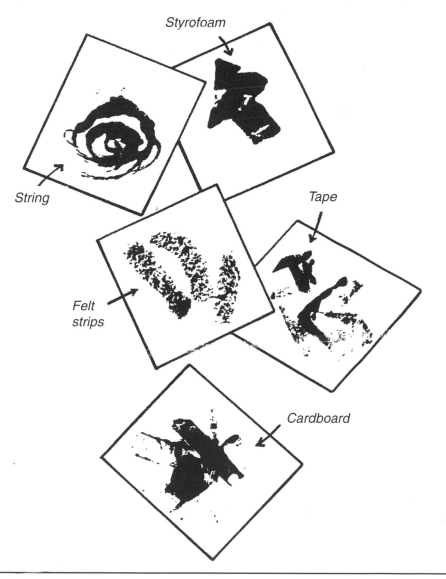

Styrofoam

String

Tape

Felt strips

Cardboard

Palette painting

Materials
- thick finger paint, many colours in muffin tins or cups
- palette knife, plastic knife, craft stick or tongue depressor
- board or cardboard
- covered table

Art process
1. Using a palette knife or palette knife substitute, spread paint on the board surface in the same way that butter is spread on toast.
2. Experiment with the end and sides of the knife for other effects.
3. Dry the artwork overnight.

Variation
- Use other tools for spreading, mixing and painting such as a cotton swab, pencil, stick, spatula or spoon.

 HINT *Palette knife painting enables the artist to see how colours mix, to experiment with stroke and design and to feel the thickness of paint and how it can be manipulated. Many young artists end up with something resembling chocolate mud on their board but this just shows how much they have enjoyed and experimented with colour mixing. Give them another board. Each experiment will yield a new appreciation and result.*

Swinging paint

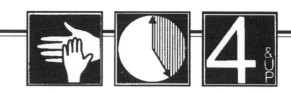

Materials
- masking tape
- large sheet of paper
- paintbrushes in a variety of sizes
- string
- ready-mixed paint, in a variety of colours in trays or tins

Art process
1. Tape a large sheet of paper to the floor.
2. Next tie strings to the handles of a variety of paintbrushes.
3. Dip the paintbrush into the paint.
4. While standing over the paper, hold the string and let the paintbrush hang down and touch the paper. Swing the paintbrush making designs as the brush dangles, swings and brushes against the paper.
5. Refill brushes with paint as needed.

Variation
- Hang other objects from strings such as a cotton swab, pencil, nuts, bolts or rubber. Dip those items in the paint and make designs on the paper with them.

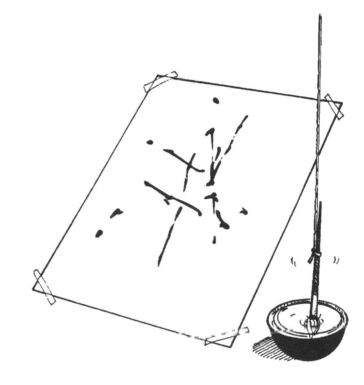

HINT *The brushes are a bit hard to control with drips and so forth. Protect the floor with plastic or newspaper.*

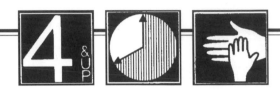

Easy pendulum paint

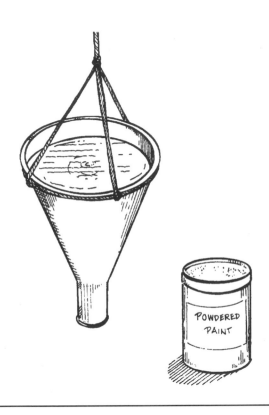

POWDERED PAINT

Materials
- small plastic funnel
- strong string
- tape
- large sheet of paper
- powdered paint
- liquid starch
- scissors
- small jug

Art process
1. An **adult** should tie a string around the large edge of a plastic funnel. Tie or tape three strings about 40 cm in length spaced equally around the edge of the funnel. Tie the three ends together above the funnel.
2. Mix liquid starch and powdered paint in a jug so that it flows smoothly, but is not too thin.
3. Hold the pendulum funnel and string over the paper.
4. Place a finger over the spout of the funnel with the other hand.
5. **Adult** pours paint in the funnel.
6. When the funnel is full, remove the finger and give the funnel a swing.
7. Keep the pendulum funnel moving until all the paint has run out of the funnel.
8. Add a new colour to the funnel and keep painting, if desired.

Variations
- Balance a dowel from one chair to another and hang the pendulum funnel from the dowel. Proceed as above by adding paint and removing the finger from the spout to release the paint.
- Fill the funnel with coloured sand, plain sand or salt and powdered paint mixed together. Proceed as above.

HINT *This project takes some coordination and timing but is great fun and creates very interesting designs.*

Paste batik

Materials
- 100 g flour
- 100 ml water
- 2 teaspoons alum
- liquidizer
- tape
- water
- scissors
- iron
- small piece of 100% cotton muslin, unlaundered
- corrugated cardboard
- several squeezy bottles
- paste food colours from cake decorating shop
- several clean, empty shallow margerine tubs
- paintbrushes

Art process
1. Mix the flour, water and alum into a paste using a liquidizer. Put some of the paste in several squeezy bottles.
2. Tape the muslin to a square of cardboard. Draw with the squeezy bottles of paste on the muslin. Try to maintain a smooth flow of paste. Dots, lines and solid masses are also effective. Dry the project overnight.
3. Mix paste food colours in shallow tins with water. A small amount will give a rich hue.
4. Dip a paintbrush into the food colour mixture and brush colour over the dry paste designs. Dry the project completely.
5. Chip and rub the dry paste off the muslin with fingers. The drawing underneath will be white.

Variation
- Make a greetings card by gluing the batik to a piece of coloured paper.

 HINT *Shallow margerine tubs are more stable than tall containers for the paste food colours.*

A large 1 x 1.5 metre piece of muslin would work well for a group project.

Salt figures

C L A Y

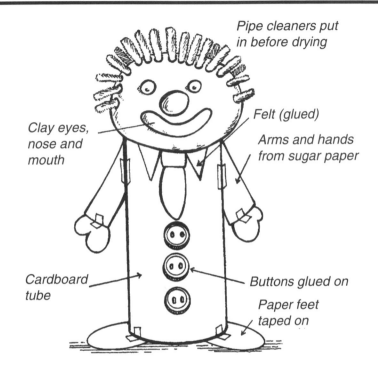

Pipe cleaners put in before drying

Clay eyes, nose and mouth

Felt (glued)

Arms and hands from sugar paper

Cardboard tube

Buttons glued on

Paper feet taped on

Materials
- salt ceramic mixture: 200 g salt, 100 g cornflour, 150 g water
- saucepan and wooden spoon
- cooker
- foil
- food colouring
- cardboard tube
- toothpicks
- decorating materials such as wool, cotton, felt, coloured paper, scraps of fabric, feathers, fabric trims or lace
- glue or tape

Art process
1. **Adult** cooks the clay ingredients over a medium heat in a saucepan. Stir with a wooden spoon until the mixture thickens into a ball. Remove from the heat and place on a piece of foil to cool. Knead the dough thoroughly.
2. Fill the cardboard tube with clay or something else heavy enough to keep it from tipping over.
3. Place a ball of clay on top of the tube for a head. Add food colouring to small bits of clay. Use the coloured clay to make facial features. If features won't stick, moisten the clay with a bit of water and then attach. Toothpicks also help features to stick to the clay.
4. Dry for several days until the head and tube filling are dry.
5. Add any decorations for clothing, hair, hats, glasses, beards, arms or plaits. Use glue or tape.

HINT

Salt ceramic clay often needs to be re-kneaded to make it smooth and pliable again.

Clay can be stored in an airtight plastic bag until ready to use.

Salt ceramic dries rock hard without being baked.

Wire sculpting

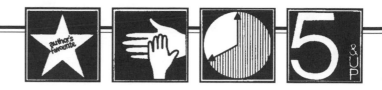

Materials
- plaster of Paris
- water
- measuring jug
- bowl
- spoon
- small milk carton
- scrap telephone cable (coloured wires inside the cable) pre-cut to 30 cm or other manageable lengths
- watercolour paints, optional
- decorative items such as beads or ribbon, optional

Art process
1. **Adult** mixes one cup of plaster of Paris with half a cup of water in a bowl with a spoon. (Note: do not rinse plaster down the sink as it may harden in the pipes.)
2. Pour plaster into the small milk carton. (There will be enough plaster for about three cartons.)
3. As the plaster begins to harden, the artist can place wires in the plaster in any fashion, number and arrangement. Dry the plaster until hard.
4. When plaster is dry and hard, tear away the milk carton. Bend and sculpt the wires into a shape or sculpture.
5. Add optional sculpture items to the wires if desired such as beads, ribbons or other items.
6. The plaster may be painted with watercolours or left white.

HINT

Telephone cable can be collected from telephone installation representatives or call the local phone company to arrange to pick up scrap wire. The outer covering of the cable can be stripped away revealing a rainbow of wires which can be cut with scissors and used for many art experiences.

Let the unused plaster harden in the mixing bowl, pop it out when dry and then wipe the bowl with a wet towel. The bowl may be washed in the sink. Hands should be washed in a bucket of soapy water rather than in the sink. Throw the water outside. Never rinse plaster down the drain because it can harden in the plumbing and cause real trouble.

SCULPTURE

Collection collage

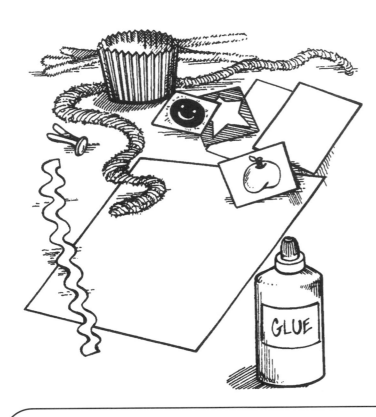

Materials
- assorted collage materials including pipe cleaners, crepe paper, paper cake cases, stickers, foil, magazine pages, fabrics, items of haberdashery, paper fasteners, feathers and wool
- PVA glue in cups with brushes
- background material such as board, cardboard, wood or heavy paper

Art process
1. Glue any assortment of collage items on the background materials.
2. Dip the brush in the cup of glue and paint the background surface; attach the object in the glue and add additional glue if necessary.
3. Form a realistic picture or a random design.

Variation
- Limit choices of material. For example, choose one decorating material and an interesting background material, such as feathers on a textured wallpaper, pompoms on colourful fabric or wool scraps on bright board.

 HINT *Stay out of the way during this project and watch the wonderful creativity of young artists.*

Candle holder

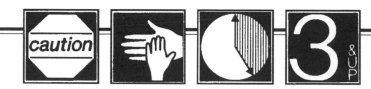

Materials
- homemade playdough (see pages 43 and 44)
- small pine cones, weeds, sticks, seed pods and nuts
- candle
- aluminium pie dish
- glitter
- silver or gold spray paint, optional
- hair grips
- ribbons

Art process
1. Playdough will form the base of the candle holder. Place a ball of playdough in the pie dish and press it down to fill the dish.
2. Push a candle into the centre of the playdough. Short, fat candle varieties work well.
3. Push other items into the playdough such as pine cones, weeds, sticks, seed pods and nuts.
4. If a silver or gold candle holder is desired, remove the candle and an **adult** sprays the candle holder outside with silver or gold paint. Glitter may be sprinkled into the wet paint. When the base is dry, replace the candle.
5. Tie ribbons or bows to hair grips and push them into the playdough too.
6. With adult supervision, light the candle briefly and then snuff it out. Never burn candles unattended because the materials in this project are flammable.

HINT

One-to-one adult supervision is necessary during the entire time the candle is lit.

A safer variation is to set a night light inside a small clear jar and place this in the playdough candle holder. The glass jar will help contain the flame.

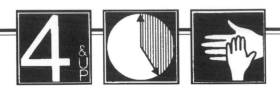

Stuffed fabric

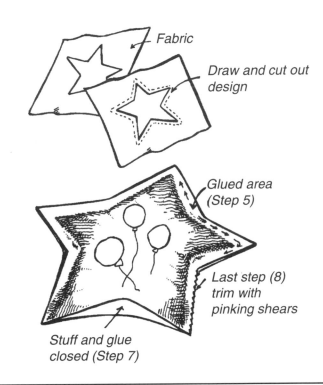

Fabric

Draw and cut out design

Glued area (Step 5)

Last step (8) trim with pinking shears

Stuff and glue closed (Step 7)

Materials
- pencil or crayon
- plain or patterned fabric squares, about 20 cm square
- scissors
- fabric pens
- fabric glue in a bottle
- stapler
- pillow stuffing or scraps for stuffing
- stapler, optional
- pinking shears

Art process
1. Draw a design or shape on the fabric. Repeat the exact design on another piece of fabric.
2. Cut the shapes out with scissors.
3. Decorate the fabric with fabric pens, if desired.
4. Place the two decorated identical shapes together, insides of fabric touching (right sides out).
5. Use fabric glue in a bottle to glue the edges together keeping one area open for stuffing. Dry the project completely or overnight.
6. Stuff the shape with fabric scraps or pillow stuffing.
7. When stuffed, glue the remaining edge of the shape. If it won't hold, staple that edge and remove staples when glue has dried.
8. Trim with pinking shears or scalloping scissors after sealing with glue and stuffing.

HINT

Fabric glues are often very different in nature. Find one that says "Fast drying" or "Good for seams".

Make stuffed toys, tree decorations or little dolls for big dolls to play with.

Sew the shape on a machine or by hand instead of gluing.

Stuffed stuff

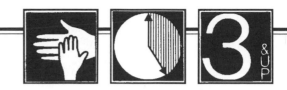

Materials
- large sheets of lining paper about 1 m square
- newspaper or other large scrap paper
- pens, crayons, paint and brushes
- stapler
- scissors
- wool

Art process
1. Choose a shape or a design such as a fish, pumpkin, animal or abstract shape.
2. Draw it very large on a sheet of lining paper.
3. An **adult** or the artist can cut out the shape from the outline. To make two shapes at once, staple two sheets together and then cut them at the same time. There will be two separate shapes.
4. Paint, draw or otherwise decorate both sides of the shape with colours, or glue additional items to decorate.
5. Staple the two sheets together at the edge. Leave an opening on one of the sides of the paper.
6. Now stuff the shape with bunched up newspaper or other scraps of paper to fill out the shape. When filled, staple the closing.
7. Add wool, if desired, to hang the finished creation from the ceiling.

Variations
- Stuff the shape with a gift, prizes, sweets, rewards or other fun items. Give this project to someone special.
- Make an entire zoo, undersea world or crazy shape garden.

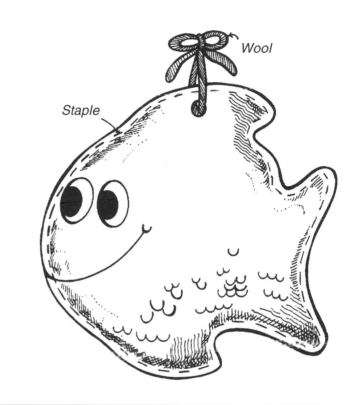

Wool

Staple

HINT *Your artists love large artwork. The stapling can be difficult, but allow the artist to do as much as possible.*

CONSTRUCTION

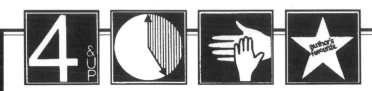

Life-size animal

Materials
- collection of large and medium cardboard boxes, cardboard tubes and other cardboard materials
- wide masking tape or duct tape
- flour and water paste in large tub or bucket
- newspaper torn in half strips
- fabric scraps, sewing scraps or coloured paper
- ready-mixed paints and paintbrushes

Art process
1. Assemble and practise "building" a cardboard animal with boxes. Do not glue, tape or otherwise secure the shape. Form the sculpture first.
2. When satisfied with the size and configuration, use wide masking tape or duct tape to hold the animal together.
3. Dip and soak a half sheet of newspaper briefly in the bucket of flour and water paste until wet and coated. Squeeze out the excess paste.
4. With bare hands, spread the sheet of newspaper over the animal shape. Press out the wrinkles with bare hands or use a small damp towel.
5. Add layers of newspaper over the box animal until completely covered. Some extra bumps, curves and features can be added with balls, lumps and mounds of soaked paper if desired.
6. Dry the sculpture several days until crunchy and hollow sounding.
7. Paint the box animal with paint or decorate with fabrics and papers.

HINT

Artists love to build something really large. The mess of working with flour and water paste and newspaper is compensated by the creativity and joy of sculpting something life-sized.

Keep a bucket of soapy water handy for washing hands.

Wood bas-relief

Materials
- wood scraps
- piece of masonite or thin plywood for background
- PVA glue
- newspaper
- paints and brushes, optional

Art process
1. Place a piece of masonite or thin plywood on the floor. (Protect the floor with newspaper if needed.)
2. Using small puddles of glue, lay wood scraps flat against the masonite (as opposed to standing straight like a building or sculpture).
3. Dry the project overnight.
4. When dry, the bas-relief can be painted with one or several colours.

Variations
- Thick wool can be glued into the relief between the scraps.
- With thinned glue add magazine pictures, wrapping paper or other paper to entirely coat and cover the pieces of wood. The artist may also choose to add more pieces of wood.
- Build a stand-up sculpture. Masking tape can help hold the sculpture while glue dries.

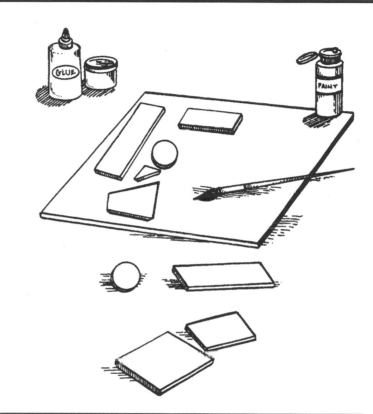

 HINT

Good sources for wood scraps include framing shops, secondary school woodwork classes, cabinet shops and construction sites.

A glue gun can be used for rapid construction and sculpting with one-to-one adult supervision.

CONSTRUCTION

Nail collage

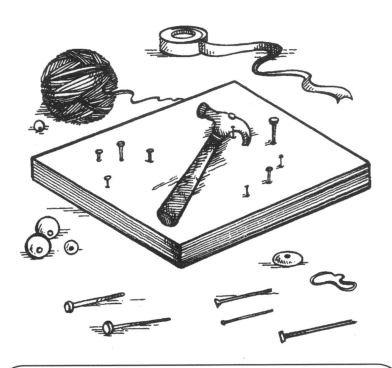

HINT

Varying the height of the nails can be effective when used as texture or design in the shape. For example, if designing a tropical fish, keep some nails low for the outside shape, fat headed nails for the scales, small headed nails for the fins and add string and wool for the tropical fish colours.

Random designs are commonly the choice of young artists rather than realistic shapes like fish.

Materials
- nails of all lengths and sizes, with heads and without
- hammer
- square of thick plywood
- woodwork or craft table
- decorative items such as wool, beads, ribbons or rubber bands
- pencil

Art process
1. Draw a simple design or object on the plywood with the pencil.
2. Nail one kind of nail into the pencilled design. Try to keep all of one kind of nail the same height.
3. Now use another type of nail on a different part of the design, keeping those about the same height.
4. Proceed with other types of nails.
5. If desired, add decorations to the design by securing them among the nails.

Variations
- Make a board with nails and use rubber bands for the designs.
- String embroidery thread from nail to nail for a spider's web effect.
- Before nailing, cover the board with glued magazine pictures, paint, wrapping paper or art tissue.

Cardboard stabile

Materials
- corrugated cardboard
- paper cutter, if possible
- scissors
- PVA glue in bottle
- covered work area
- paint and brushes, optional
- masking tape, optional

Art process
1. **Adult** cuts geometric shapes such as triangles, rectangles and squares from corrugated cardboard about 7 to 12 cm each in size. Use a paper cutter to save time and sore fingers.
2. Cut a small notch or slit in one of the sides of each piece.
3. Push the two pieces together, notch to notch.
4. Add a drop of glue to make the two pieces stay together.
5. Join on another pair of cardboard shapes in this way. Continue joining pairs of cardboard shapes. You may use a piece of masking tape to help the cardboard stick.
6. Completely dry overnight or for two days.
7. Now join pairs with other pairs, cutting and gluing the notches as before. Create a small or even a very large sculpture. Dry again.
8. Remove masking tape or leave as it is. Paint the sculpture when dry, if desired.

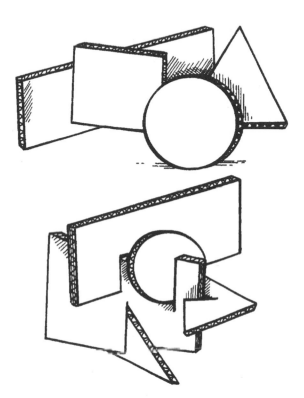

 HINT Sculptures need balance or they will fall over. Sometimes when a sculpture falls over it becomes a completely new motivation in its shape for the artist.

Stabiles are a great group project.

CONSTRUCTION

Lace rubbing

D
R
A
W
I
N
G

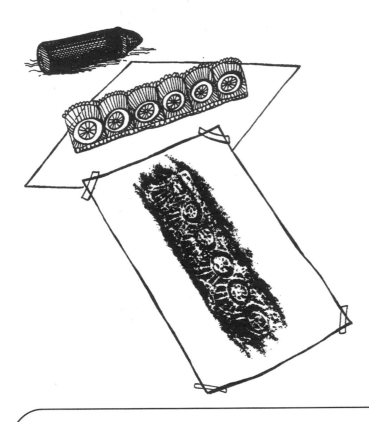

Materials
- jumbo crayons, peeled
- scraps of lace, fabric or plastic cut into hearts, squares, circles, strips or any shapes
- white drawing paper
- masking tape, optional

Art process
1. Select lace shapes and place them on the table. Place a loop of masking tape on the backs of the shapes, if desired, and stick them to the table.
2. Place a sheet of white drawing paper over the shapes. You may tape the corners of the paper to the table to help keep the paper wiggle-free.
3. Rub peeled crayons back and forth over the shapes under the paper. A rubbing will emerge.

Variation
- Move shapes around, change colours, try new shapes, make greetings cards or cut-out shapes to hang in the window or from the ceiling.

HINT

Help the artist draw or trace a heart shape.

Children's rubbings are not always like an adult's. Very young children are just learning the idea of rubbing and to control the crayon. Be patient.

Baked stubs

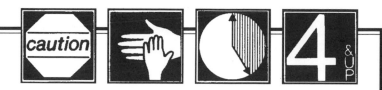

Materials
- old crayon stubs, peeled
- board or cardboard
- baking tray covered with foil
- stones, shells, felt squares, pieces of wood and other items
- hot sunny day or 250ºF (130 ºC) oven
- craft sticks or coffee stir sticks

Art process
1. Peel the paper from old broken crayons.
2. Place the board or cardboard on the covered baking tray.
3. Place peeled crayons on the board, randomly or by sticking them.
4. Add stones or shells in and around the crayons if desired.
5. Leave the arrangement in the hot sun to melt, or an **adult** should place the baking tray in a 250ºF (130 ºC) over for about ten minutes.
6. An **adult** should remove the hot sheet from the oven.
7. The artist may wish to push the melted crayon about with the craft sticks before the melted design cools. Stones, shells and other items can be pushed into the melted crayon.
8. Cool the design completely. Remove it from the baking tray.

Variation
- Melt crayon stubs on felt squares, fabric scraps, thin boards, cardboard or other sturdy papers or materials.

HINT *An adult should do all the "hot" steps such as placing the tray in the over and removing it from the oven. For safety reasons, be sure the tray is reasonably cool before the child pokes at the melted crayons.*

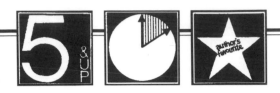

Chalk rub

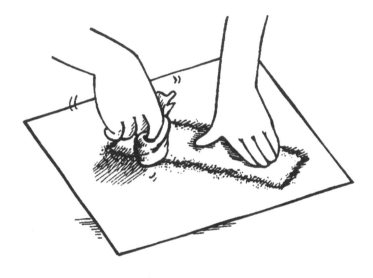

Materials
- scrap paper
- coloured chalk
- sugar paper, light colours
- facial tissues

Art process
1. Tear scrap paper into any pieces or shapes.
2. Rub chalk on the edges of the paper shapes.
3. Place the chalked shapes on light coloured sugar paper and hold with the non-drawing hand.
4. Brush the chalk from the edge of the torn paper and out on to the sugar paper with the facial tissue. This creates a stencil with blurred edges.
5. See page 158 "Three heart stencils" for a different technique.

HINT

Chalky hands and fingers are a natural result of creating with chalk.

Artists tend to want to use a new piece of tissue for each chalk rub shape, but encourage using one piece for the entire creation.

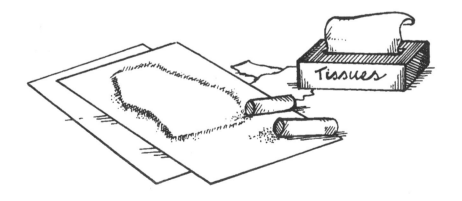

Crayon-chalk transfer

Materials
- coloured chalk (soft variety called pastels)
- 2 crayons (one white, one any other colour)
- square of board or cardboard (13 cm x 13 cm)
- sheet of smooth paper
- masking tape, optional
- blunt pencil or paintbrush handle

Art process
1. Apply chalk colours heavily to the board or cardboard. Tap the board to remove dust. Cover the whole board or just certain parts.
2. Colour with the white crayon over the chalk colours. This step takes lots of muscles and determination.
3. Coat the white crayon with any other colour crayon. Again this needs even more muscles and determination.
4. Place the sheet of smooth paper on top of the coloured board. Tape down to hold with masking tape.
5. Draw on the smooth paper with a blunt pencil or a paintbrush handle (press firmly). The chalk and crayon will transfer from the board to the smooth paper.

Variations
- Experiment with textures of board, colours of paper and types of chalk.
- Do this project on patterned paper or a watercolour painting which has dried.

 HINT *Chalk breaks and blurs easily. This is the natural condition of chalk and is nothing to worry about.*

Motivated young artists enjoy the challenge of all the colouring and covering. Some young artists tire easily or may not be as artistically driven to complete this project.

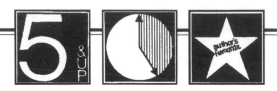

D R A W I N G

Three heart stencils

Method 3   Crayon stencil pattern

1. Place the stencil cut from the old file folder on a sheet of paper (or use the hole). Trace around it with crayon.
2. Now move the stencil slightly, overlapping the stencil on the design just traced. Trace the new location of the stencil. Use any colours. Keep moving the stencil and tracing it until the design looks like it has moved across the paper or in a pattern.

HINT *Young artists often need help drawing and cutting hearts. Sometimes it helps to have a shape to trace or simply let the child design a shape. Most artists want a heart; in this case, help may be needed to make the heart shapes only.*

Materials
- old file folders
- paper towels or tissues
- coloured chalk
- scissors
- crayons
- sugar paper
- felt pens

Art process
Cut heart shapes (or any shapes) from the old file folders using scissors. Shapes can be drawn first or cut free hand. Keep both the shape and the hole left in the folder from the cut shape.

Method 1   Chalk stencil

1. Place a shape cut from a file folder (or the hole left in the file folder) on a sheet of paper. White works well. Use the chalk to draw around or inside the shape.
2. While still holding the shape in place, brush the chalk marks with a tissue or paper towel, blurring the lines and softening the colour. Now remove the shape and see the designs left behind.

Method 2   Felt pen fingers

1. Place the hole made from a cut stencil on a sheet of paper. Colour one finger tip with felt pen until the pad of the finger is very bright.
2. Press the coloured finger on to the paper which shows through the hole. Let the print overlap on to the stencil around the hole. Fill the entire shape with fingerprints. Remove the stencil and look at the design left behind.

Tissue stain

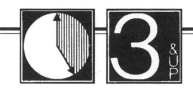

Materials
- coloured tissue paper, 3 or 4 colours torn into small bits
- board or cardboard
- paintbrushes
- water in cups
- spray bottles filled with water
- covered table

Art process
1. Place torn bits of coloured tissue paper on the board or cardboard. Several colours or just one colour can be used.
2. Spray water on the tissue pieces. Use a wet paintbrush to enhance the staining from the tissues.
3. Remove or peel away the wet tissue pieces and a stained design will be left behind.
4. Dry the project completely.
5. Add more colours after the design has dried if desired.

Variations
- Do this project on hard boiled eggs, white fabric, paper towels, coffee filters, napkins or white tissue paper.
- Cut the base in a festive or theme shape, such as a heart for Valentine's Day.

HINT *Fingers become stained too, so have a bucket of soapy warm water and a towel handy. Sometimes it takes several days for the stain to wear away.*

PAINTING

Tissue colour paint

Materials
- art tissues in many colours
- paintbrushes
- cups of water
- paper (white works well)

Art process
1. Tear or cut tissues into small pieces and shapes.
2. Place the tissue pieces in the cups of water and stir with paintbrushes.
3. When the water is coloured, paint with the coloured water on paper.

Variation
- Using liquid starch, attach tissue pieces to white paper. Dip a paintbrush into clear water and paint over the tissue pieces so that the colour spreads out on to the paper.

HINT *Use margerine tubs or pet food dishes with straight sides for containers of water that will not tip over or spill.*

Foil painting

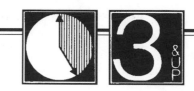

Materials
- aluminium foil
- board or cardboard
- tape, optional
- 115 ml thick paint in a cup
- 1 teaspoon washing-up liquid
- paintbrushes

Art process
1. Cover a piece of board or cardboard with aluminium foil, folding the foil around the back of the board.
2. Tape the foil if desired.
3. Add one teaspoon of washing-up liquid to the thick paint.
4. Paint on the foil. Let the project dry.

Variation
- Cover a box, bottle or picture frame with foil. Paint as above.

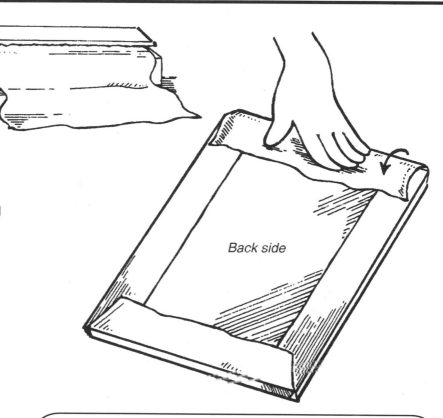

Back side

HINT *The washing-up liquid helps the paint adhere to foil, plastic or other glossy surfaces. If it isn't sticking, add another half a teaspoon of washing-up liquid to the paint.*

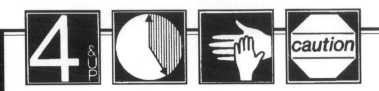

Sprinkle paint

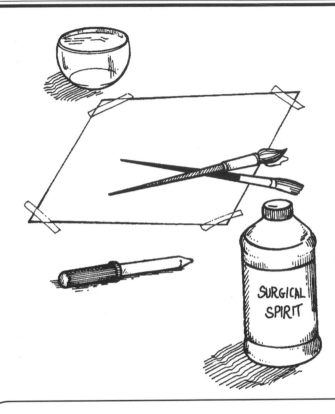

Materials
- heavy paper taped to table with masking tape
- brushes
- water
- watercolour paints
- surgical spirit or methylated spirits
- eyedroppers
- rock salt or table salt

Art process
1. Brush water all over the heavy paper until covered.
2. Paint with watercolours on the wet paper.
3. **Adult** helps drip surgical spirit from the eyedropper on the paper and then sprinkle the painting with salt. Closely supervise this step.
4. Dry the artwork completely.
5. Brush off the salt when dry.
6. Carefully remove the tape and lift the paper from the table.

HINT

The alcohol and salt cause an unusual artistic effect. However, the alcohol can be omitted in Step 3, still sprinkling the work with salt.

Use big brushes that hold lots of water to wet paper.

Dry the painting in place rather than removing it to another area.

Stamp a doodle

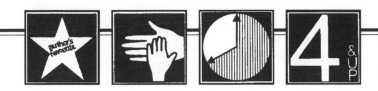

Materials
- styrofoam cup
- play clay or plasticine
- variety of printing materials such as beads, corks, small tiles, buttons or other objects
- plaster of Paris mixed to creamy consistency
- ready-mixed paint
- paper towel in styrofoam tray
- paintbrush or spoon for spreading paint
- paper

Art process
1. Cut the cup in half. Use the bottom half of the cup.
2. Press some clay into the bottom of the cup.
3. Push various little items into the clay.
4. **Adult** pours plaster of Paris into the cup until it is about 2.5 cm deep.
5. When the plaster has hardened and dried, take it out of the cup. Also remove the clay.
6. The plaster section is the stamp.
7. Pour some paint on the paper towel in the styrofoam tray.
8. Spread the paint with a brush or a spoon.
9. Press the stamp into the paint and then press it on a piece of paper to make a self-created stamp print.

Variation
- Use the stamp prints to make wrapping paper, greetings cards, wallpaper or stationery.

 HINT

Plaster hardens quickly so have everything ready to go when it's time to pour the plaster.

Although fairly involved, this project makes very interesting stamps and is worth the time and trouble.

P
A
I
N
T
I
N
G

Sugar clay

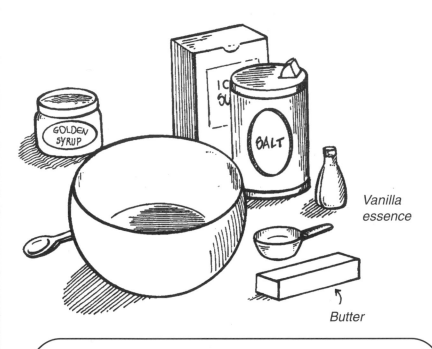

Vanilla essence

Butter

Materials
- 70 g of butter or margerine
- 75 ml golden syrup
- 1/2 teaspoon salt
- 1 teaspoon of vanilla essence
- 450 g icing sugar
- bowl
- measuring jug and spoons
- clean work surface
- spatula or knife
- food colouring
- paper towels
- plain digestive biscuits

Art process
1. Wash hands and work surface.
2. Mix the butter or margerine, golden syrup, salt and vanilla essence in a bowl with the hands.
3. Mix in the icing sugar. Knead the dough until smooth.
4. Add more icing sugar if necessary to make the clay non-sticky and pliable.
5. Divide the clay into small portions and mix in food colours or paste food dye. Use a spatula or spreading knife to mix the colours.
6. Work with bits of the coloured clay on a paper towel and decorate a plain digestive biscuit.
7. Eat your creation!

Variation
- Prepare a butter cream icing and decorate a cake, fairy cakes or digestive biscuits and then place the sugar clay designs on their icing background.

HINT *There should be enough clay from this batch for a group of thirty to decorate one digestive biscuit or fairy cake each or for one artist to decorate thirty biscuits or cakes.*

Do not make sugar clay on a hot day or the butter will melt and make the clay too sticky.

Upright sculptures such as standing animals or people won't work; flat figures and designs are best.

Apple heart pizza

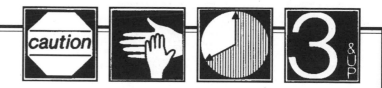

Materials
- 450 g flour
- 3/4 cup butter, room temperature
- 3 tablespoons, and 1 teaspoon sugar
- 1/4 teaspoon salt
- 150 ml cold water
- 3 medium-sized eating apples
- 1/2 teaspoon cinnamon
- oven at 400ºF (200 ºC)

- spatula
- baking tray
- chopping board
- mats
- large mixing bowl
- medium mixing bowl
- rolling pin
- apple peeler/corer

Art process
The dough:
1. In a large mixing bowl, mix the flour and butter with fingers until the flour looks a little yellow.
2. Add three tablespoons of sugar and 1/4 teaspoon salt to the flour, blending with the hands.
3. Add the cold water and continue to blend with the hands until the dough forms a ball.
4. Spread a little flour on a chopping board. Knead the dough on the floured board for five minutes. Add more flour if needed.
5. Shape the dough into a ball. Divide the ball into four equal pieces. Roll each piece with the rolling pin about 5 mm thick. Sprinkle flour on the dough to keep it from sticking.
6. Shape each piece into a flat heart shape by hand. Slide a spatula under the dough and place it on the baking tray. Do the same for the other three pieces.

The apple pizza:
1. Core and peel the apples. Cut them into four quarters and then slice each quarter into about six to ten pieces.
2. Place all the slices in a medium bowl. Sprinkle with one teaspoon of sugar and the cinnamon. Toss the apples, cinnamon and sugar until evenly coated.
3. Place the apple slices on each heart of dough in a pinwheel shape or any other design.
4. Bake for 15 minutes at 400ºF (200 ºC). When the edge is golden brown, the apple pizza hearts are ready. **Adult** removes the pizzas from the oven.
5. Slide each pizza on to a plate. Eat hot, warm or cool.

HINT *The dough can be rolled out ahead of time and keep covered in the fridge until ready to add the apples and bake.*

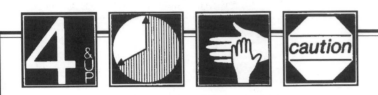

Stained glass biscuits

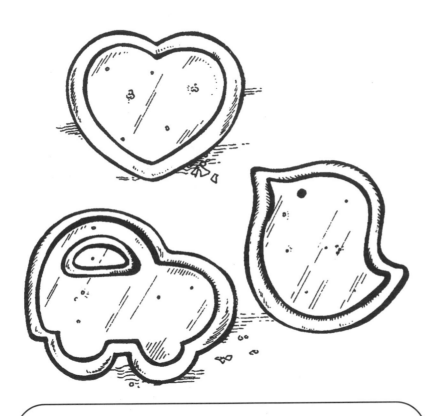

Materials
- 70 g vegetable fat
- 70 g sugar
- 1 egg
- 600 g flour with 1/2 teaspoon bicarbonate of soda added
- 1 scant teaspoon salt, optional
- 150 ml honey
- bowl
- measuring jug and spoons
- crushed lollipops or boiled sweets
- aluminium foil covered baking tray
- oven at 375ºF (190 ºC)

Art process
1. Wash hands before beginning. Mix the first six ingredients to make the biscuit dough with your hands in a bowl.
2. Roll the dough into snake shapes about 5 mm fat for the outlines of the biscuits.
3. Use the dough rolls to make biscuit designs on aluminium foil on a baking tray. Make any free-form designs, hearts, circles, cars, birds, faces or other ideas. Be sure to connect ends of the dough rolls like the outlines of a picture.
4. Sprinkle the coloured crushed sweets into the spaces of the biscuits, filling the spaces completely and heaping slightly.
5. Bake the biscuits at 375ºF (190 ºC) for 8–10 minutes.
6. **Adult** removes the biscuits from the oven to cool. When dough is cool and firm, gently peel off the aluminium foil from the stained glass biscuit. Delicious when cool!

HINT

If adding sticks, be sure the oven is big enough or biscuits are small enough to fit in the oven once the stick is added.

Experiment with colours of crushed sweets, although red always seems to be the favourite.

Tissue contact

Materials
- clear, contact paper
- art tissue, variety of colours
- scissors
- hole punch
- wool
- optional collage items such as bits of lace, thread, confetti, glitter or hole punches

Art process
1. Cut a rectangle of clear contact paper about 15 cm x 30 cm or any other size.
2. Fold the rectangle in half. Peel the backing halfway off the back, stopping at the fold.
3. Lay the clear side of the clear contact paper on the table, sticky side up.
4. Using any little torn or cut pieces of art tissue, attach them to the sticky contact paper. No glue is necessary. Festive shapes such as hearts or flowers can also be used.
5. When the design is complete, pull the remainder of the contact paper backing off.
6. Fold over the remaining contact paper and stick it to the design.
7. Take scissors and trim the ragged edges.
8. If desired, punch a hole in the top of the design, add a piece of wool and hang the artwork in a window or near a light source.

Variation
- Cut the finished contact paper design into a heart shape for a pretty Valentine card.

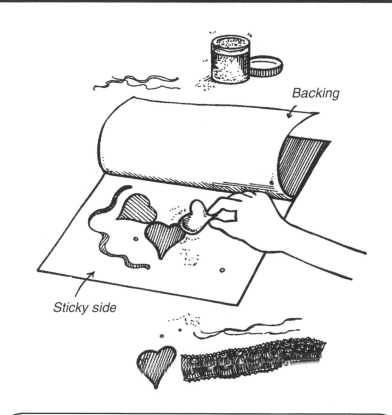

Backing

Sticky side

HINT *The folding steps can be very wrinkly and off-centre depending on the ages and abilities of the artists. Accept this outcome.*

Heart à l'art

COLLAGE

Materials
- variety of papers—wrapping paper, magazine pictures, coloured paper, tissue paper, poster or book jackets
- scissors
- glue
- board or cardboard
- crayons, felt pens, paints or any drawing/colouring tools
- heart-shaped stencils or patterns

Art process
1. Trace heart-shaped patterns or stencils on any variety of papers or draw hearts freehand.
2. Cut out the shapes. Use the heart-shaped holes left from the hearts too.
3. Begin gluing hearts on the board or cardboard in any design or pattern desired.
4. Add drawings with pen or crayon on the board too, if desired.
5. Some artists like to fill the entire board with hearts, while others prefer a simple approach.

Variation
- Use the hearts for Valentine cards, mobiles, posters or wall decorations.

HINT

Hearts are often difficult to draw but are so enjoyed by young children that stencils and patterns are fun to use once in a while.

Heart flutters

Materials

- one sheet of greaseproof paper, folded and opened
- PVA glue in a dish, thinned with water until milky
  (and a few drops of liquid detergent to prevent beading)
- big paintbrush
- art tissue
- scissors
- newspaper-covered table
- hole punch
- wool or rubber bands

Art process

1. Brush thinned PVA glue on half of the greaseproof paper.
2. Stick heart shapes or pieces and patterns of torn or cut art tissue in any colours all over the sticky greaseproof paper. Valentine colours would be effective for a fluttery decoration.
3. Brush more PVA glue over the hearts and tissue designs.
4. Fold the rest of the greaseproof paper over the design.
5. Dry overnight.
6. Cut the dry tissue collage into long skinny shapes or strips—snakes, lightning or other shapes.
7. Punch a hole in the top of each strip.
8. Loop a rubber band or piece of wool through the hole.
9. Hang the heart flutters from a stick, a hanger or from pins in the frames around a window.

Variations

- Make bookmarks instead of flutters.
- Frame the tissue collage instead of cutting it into strips.

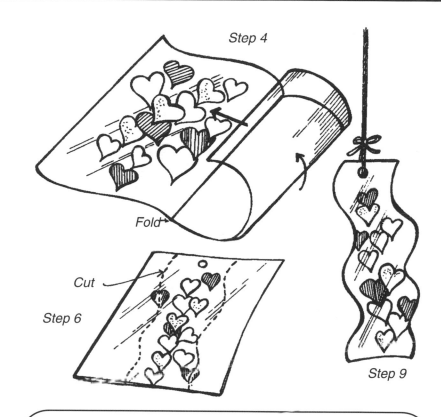

Step 4

Fold

Cut

Step 6

Step 9

HINT Punch the hole at least 1 cm from the end to prevent tearing.

Expect the wet glue to look cloudy; it will dry clear.

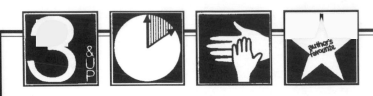

Sewing cards

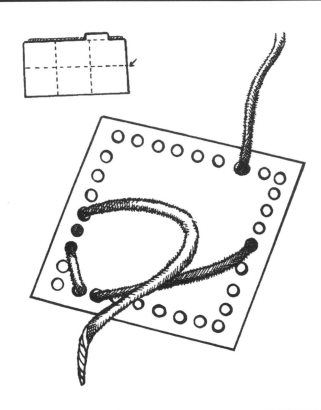

Materials
- old file folders
- heavy cord, wool or coloured string in pre-cut lengths
- paper punch
- scissors
- masking tape
- crayons or felt pens

Art process
1. Cut the old file folders into 15 cm x 15 cm squares or any other shapes.
2. Use the paper punch to make holes around the edges of the shape.
3. Tape the end of the wool with masking tape to make a darning needle-like point.
4. Tape the other end of the wool to the back of the shape. Begin sewing the wool through the holes and making any shapes, designs or patterns desired.
5. When the wool runs out, tape the end to the back of the board and continue with a new piece or new colour.
6. When the sewing is complete, colour in between where the wools cross over making triangles, squares and other shapes. Use crayon, felt pen or both.

Variations
- Complete this project on styrofoam grocery trays or paper plates shaped in designs such as hearts, flowers, cars or cats.
- Have pre-punched materials for the artists to sew.
- Use heart-shaped materials for Valentine's sewing cards.

HINT

If punching the holes is too difficult for the artist, an adult can take directions and punch the holes as the artist directs.

A heavy-duty hole punch is sharper and cuts through thicker paper with ease.

Easy tubescope

Materials
- cardboard tube, any diameter from small to large
- greaseproof paper
- art tissue scraps
- hole punch
- scissors
- PVA glue thinned with water
- paintbrush
- tape or heavy rubber band

Art process
1. Cut a piece of greaseproof paper into a circle 3–5 cm larger than the end of the cardboard tube.
2. Using the paintbrush dipped in thin glue, brush bits of art tissue on the greaseproof paper circle. Pieces can be torn, cut with scissors, or little circles made with a hole punch can be used.
3. Dry the greaseproof paper, glue and tissue overnight.
4. When dry, place the edges over the edges of the tube. Tape the greaseproof paper circle to the tube or use a heavy rubber band.
5. Look through the other end of the tube to see the colours and designs. Hold the colours up to the light too.

Variations
- Use cling film or cellophane instead of greaseproof paper.
- Cover the other end of the tube with cellophane.

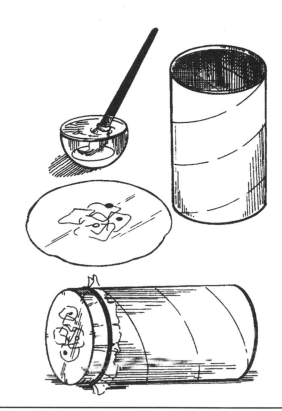

 HINT *Young artists often like to look through coloured cellophane, tissues and papers before sticking them to the greaseproof paper so they can decide which colours are most effective for them to use on their own tubescope.*

CRAFT

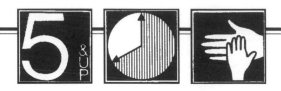

String snacks

Materials
- embroidery thread or crochet thread
- scissors
- large-eyed plastic needle
- food items—dry cereal with holes, raisins, prunes, dried apricots or fruit gums
- beads from from baked bread dough

Art process
1. Thread the needle. Knot the doubled thread at one end.
2. String various food items on the thread until the string is full.
3. Cut the end of the string at the needle and tie this end to the other end of the string making a complete circle, necklace or garland of food.
4. Wear, eat and enjoy! A real portable snack!

Variations
- String a small box of raisins to the necklace as a pendant.
- Fill squares of cling film with seeds or nuts and attach these to the necklace too.
- Use patterns in the design such as dark/light, smooth/rough or large/small.
- Go for a walk while wearing snack necklaces.
- Make the necklaces for gifts.

HINT

Expect some snacking while creating.

Wash hands before beginning this activity.

Colourful stir sticks

Materials
- wooden coffee stir sticks
- powdered dye or food colouring
- warm water in baking pan
- paper towels, newspaper
- masking tape
- tongs or wide spatula

Art process
1. Mix powdered dye or food colouring in the warm water in the baking pan. Make several pans of different colours, if desired.
2. Place wooden stir sticks in the warm dye.
3. Remove the sticks with the tongs or a spatula and place on the newspaper to dry. Drying takes several hours or overnight.
4. When dry, build a sculpture by taping the stir sticks together with bits of masking tape.

Variation
- For a festive or Valentine theme, glue little paper hearts or lace to the finished sculpture.

HINT

A warm dye mixture colours the wood faster than a cool mixture.

The dye also colours hands and fingers, so wear rubber gloves or use tongs to lift the wet sticks out of the dye.

Dye match sticks, craft sticks or other wooden items to use for sculpture.

CONSTRUCTION

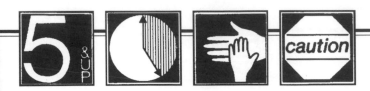

caution

King size rope wrap

Materials
- rope, wool, string or cord
- square of plywood at least 1.5 cm thick and 70 cm square (or larger)
- hammer
- nail with large heads, 1.5 cm or less in length
- optional—feathers, cotton wool balls, ribbon or other decorative odds and ends.

Art process
1. Hammer nails into the plywood square in any design. Nails can go around the edge, or may be hammered into the centre. An **adult** should carefully supervise this step and watch to see that nails do not go all the way through the plywood and into the floor or table.
2. When there are sufficient nails, tape rope or wool and begin winding, wrapping, tying and weaving around the various nails to form colourful designs.
3. Add optional decorations to the wool or rope as desired.

Variations
- Make this a group project with an even larger sheet of plywood, more nails and more artists working together.
- Paint the wood background first.
- Cover the wood with wrapping paper or contact paper first.

HINT
Some artists need help tying the wools and rope around the nails. Masking tape can also help.

Spring

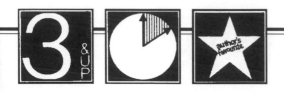

Tape and chalk stencil

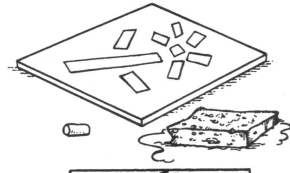

Materials
- masking tape
- board or cardboard
- damp sponge
- coloured chalk

Art process
1. Apply masking tape to the board or cardboard in any design.
2. Rub chalk on a damp sponge or draw designs on a damp sponge.
3. Press the chalked sponge all over the taped board or cardboard. The chalk will stick to the paper.
4. Peel off the masking tape and a stencil design from the tape will be left.

Variations
- This same project can be done with masking tape and watercolour paint. Paint the paper or board with watercolour paints instead of the chalk. Peel off the tape and a negative design will be left.
- Cut the masking tape in shapes.
- Use clear contact paper instead of masking tape.

HINT

Do not leave tape on the paper too long or it will not come off.

Leave a little edge of tape sticking up and it will be easier to peel off.

Sandpaper melt

Materials
- electric warming tray covered in foil
- peeled crayons
- sandpaper, medium grade
- thick work gloves to protect hands

Art process
1. Place the sandpaper on the heated warming tray.
2. Wear a thick work glove on the non-drawing hand to protect against burns while holding the sandpaper down.
3. Slowly draw or rub the peeled crayon over the heated sandpaper.
4. Remove the sandpaper from the warming tray when the design is complete. The drawing will cool and harden.

Variation
- Draw on typing paper, drawing paper or experiment with other papers on the warming tray.

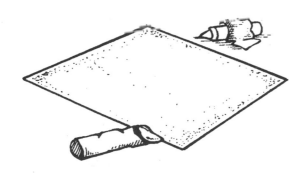

> **HINT**
>
> Tape the corners of the sandpaper to the surface of the warming tray to prevent paper from wiggling.
>
> Keep the warming tray on a table against a wall and tape the cord to the table to prevent artists tripping over cord.
>
> Observe caution with the warming tray. One-to-one supervision is necessary for projects involving heat.

DRAWING

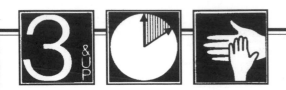

Fabric starched chalk

Materials
- square of cotton fabric
- liquid starch in a bucket or bowl
- tray
- water
- coloured chalk

Art process
1. Soak cotton fabric in the bowl of liquid starch.
2. Wring out the fabric with your hands.
3. Place the fabric on a tray and smooth out the wrinkles.
4. Use coloured chalk to draw on the wet fabric.
5. Dry the artwork in place or remove to another drying area and dry flat.

Variations
- Work with a textured surface under the fabric so chalk will pick up the design of the texture underneath the fabric.
- Frame the completed design or display in an embroidery hoop.

HINT

The chalk will be brighter when moistened by the starch. It will stay on the fabric better than a dry fabric and chalk art project.

Do not wash this fabric or the design will wash out.

DRAWING

Layered colour muffins

Materials

- old crayons, peeled and separated by colour
- frying pan covered with aluminium foil
- metal cup or small pan (lined with foil), a muffin tin, metal ice cube tray, or chocolate mould
- oven gloves

Art process

1. Place one colour of crayon pieces in a metal cup in the hot frying pan.
2. Melt the crayon until liquid.
3. Pour a thin layer of melted crayon into a mould. Cool completely.
4. Melt another colour of crayon.
5. Pour a thin layer of the second colour on top of the first colour. Cool completely.
6. Continue to layer colours of melted crayon until mould is full.
7. When completely cool, pop the layered crayon muffin out of the mould and use to colour on paper.

> **HINT**
>
> *Cool the crayon layers in the freezer for quick results.*
>
> *Observe caution in all steps involving the heated frying pan. This project requires one-to-one supervision with an adult to prevent injury or burns.*

DRAWING

Sandpaper print

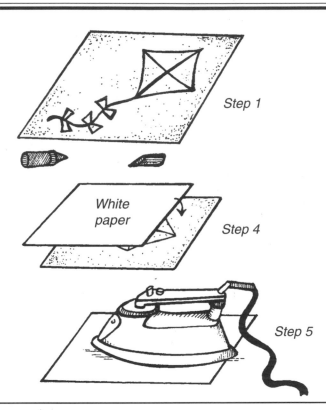

Step 1

White paper

Step 4

Step 5

Materials
- sandpaper, medium grade
- crayons
- newspaper
- old iron, very warm
- white paper

Art process
1. Draw on the sandpaper with crayons, pressing hard.
2. Place a thick pad of newspaper on a table where the iron is set up to press.
3. Carry sandpaper to ironing area.
4. Cover the sandpaper with a sheet of white paper.
5. **Adult** irons the white paper on the sandpaper, allowing the crayon marks to melt on to the white paper.
6. To make several prints of the same crayon design, re-colour the design with crayons and press again with the iron on a new sheet of white paper.

HINT

This is a great way to produce several copies of prints by one child.

Some children will be able to do the ironing with supervision. Work at a low table.

Tape sandpaper to the table so it won't wiggle while the artist is drawing.

Print from sandpaper drawing

Glossy paint

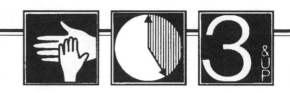

Materials
- one tin sweetened condensed milk
- 4 colours food colouring
- 4 cups
- white drawing paper
- paintbrushes
- cotton swabs
- bulletin board
- drawing pins

Art process
1. Cut shapes from the white drawing paper or draw shapes on the paper.
2. Mix a different colour of food colouring with condensed milk in each of the four cups.
3. Use a paintbrush or a cotton swab to paint the shapes in different colours.
4. While the paint is still wet, hang the shapes on a wall with drawing pins so the paint colours will run together. (A fence or bulletin board works too.)
5. Dry the art for several days.

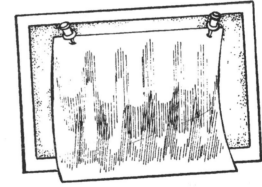

Variations
- Use this paint idea for painting or designing eggs for Easter or spring themes.
- Mix a combination of bright colours and pastel colours.

HINT

You may need to help young children carry the painted shape, push in pins and keep control of the project.

Cover the floor beneath the dripping paint.

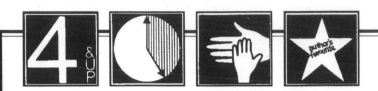

Cornflour paint

*1 teaspoon
vinegar*

*1 teaspoon
cornflour*

*20 drops of food
colouring*

Materials
- teaspoon
- baby food jar with lid
- vinegar
- cornflour
- food colouring
- paper
- paintbrush

Art process
1. Mix one teaspoon vinegar, one teaspoon cornflour and twenty drops of food colouring in the baby food jar.
2. Shake the ingredients to mix.
3. Make several different colours in separate jars.
4. Dip a paintbrush into the cornflour paint and paint on paper as with ready-mixed paint.

Variations
- Paint on hard boiled eggs.
- Paint on wood scraps.
- Experiment with painting on other surfaces.

 HINT *You may double or triple this recipe if you need a large supply of this paint.*

Substitute cream or paste food colouring found in cake decorating shops for a brighter paint that goes further.

Food colouring can stain clothing, so have soapy water and towels ready. Cover children and table surfaces to prevent spills

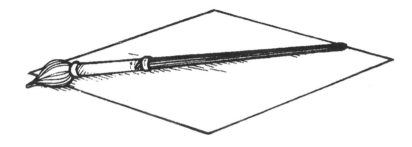

Rolled egg

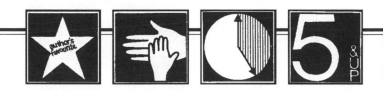

Materials
- small baking tin
- ready-mixed paints, several colours
- hard-boiled eggs
- paper to fit pan
- cooling rack
- empty egg carton

Art process
1. Place the paper in the bottom of the baking tin. Trim the paper to fit if necessary.
2. Pour several colours of paint on the paper.
3. Place the egg in the tin.
4. Gently tip the tin and roll the egg through the paints. Tip the tin very slightly and gently or the egg will crash into sides of baking tin.
5. Dry the egg on wire mesh or a cooling rack. The paint can rub off the egg on clothes and hands, especially wet hands, so carry dry eggs in an egg carton.

Variation
- The paper from the bottom of the pan can be an art project, too.

HINT

Sit down during the tipping stage.

For very young children, use a small plastic container instead of a baking tin.

Use food colouring mixed in half a cup of water with one tablespoon of vinegar instead of paint for egg designs that aren't quite as thick as paint.

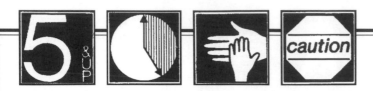

Batik eggs

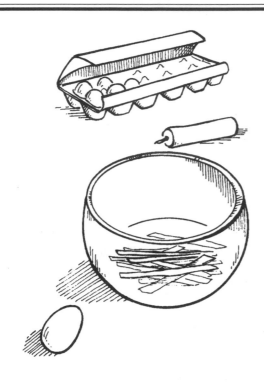

Materials
- egg carton or wrinkled aluminum foil for egg drying rack
- hard-boiled eggs
- crepe paper, several colours
- scissors
- bowl
- hot water
- tweezers
- 1 tablespoon white vinegar
- candle, matches
- paper towels
- covered table

Art process
1. Cut strips of crepe paper about 1–1.5 cm wide. Place them in a bowl. Do the same for additional colours of crepe paper.
2. **Adult** pours hot water on the crepe paper to release the dye. Remove the paper with tweezers or fingers.
3. Add a tablespoon of white vinegar to set the dye. Let cool.
4. **Adult** drips candle wax on to any area of the egg to leave the surface of the egg its natural colour.
5. Eggs will be decorated with several applications of wax and dye. Start by dipping the egg in the lightest colour of dye first. Dry the egg with a paper towel.
6. **Adult** drips more candle wax on to the parts of the egg the artist wishes to keep a light colour of dye. Dip the egg into the next darker dye and dry with a paper towel. (It may take a few minutes for the dye to become the desired colour.)
7. To remove the wax, an **adult** places the egg on a tray covered with paper towels in a very warm oven. After the wax has melted (in about two minutes), wipe the egg with another paper towel. Cool in an egg carton or on wrinkled aluminium foil.

HINT

This is one of those projects where the adult ends up doing most of the work. Let the child do as much as possible. This is a one-to-one project.

Fresh eggs can be emptied by poking a pin hole in both ends of the egg and blowing out the contents with a hefty puff of air. The contents can be used for cooking. This leaves a fragile but light, empty egg for dyeing. This egg can then be kept indefinitely.

Onion skin egg

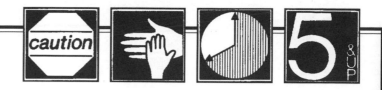

Materials

- uncooked eggs
- brown or purple onion skins
- squares of old cloth or nylon stockings
- small leaves or rice
- rubber bands
- pot for boiling eggs
- cooker
- paper towels
- covered table
- cooking oil

Art process

1. Place the cloth or nylon stocking square on the table.
2. Put about six layers of onion skin on the cloth.
3. Place leaves or bits of rice on top of the onion skins. Put more onion skins on top of those.
4. Place the egg on top of the skins, leaves or rice. Place more onion skins on top of this.
5. Wrap the cloth or nylon stocking around the egg and skins firmly. Wrap several rubber bands around the cloth to keep it in place and to press the onion skins firmly against the egg's surface.
6. **Adult** lowers the wrapped egg into a pot of boiling water for about 30 minutes.
7. Remove the egg from the pot and cool.
8. Remove the cloth and materials from the egg.
9. Rub the egg with a little cooking oil to give it a shine.

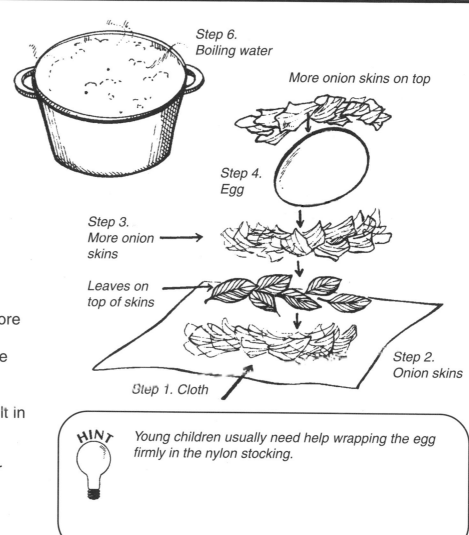

Step 6.
Boiling water

More onion skins on top

Step 4.
Egg

Step 3.
More onion skins

Leaves on top of skins

Step 2.
Onion skins

Step 1. Cloth

HINT *Young children usually need help wrapping the egg firmly in the nylon stocking.*

PAINTING

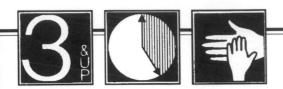

SCULPTURE

Plastic bag art

Materials
- plaster of Paris
- water
- plastic sandwich bag
- powdered paints
- ready-mixed paints, optional
- paintbrushes, optional
- wooden block or piece of board for a base, optional

Art process
1. Scoop some plaster of Paris into a plastic sandwich bag.
2. Add a tablespoon or more of powdered paint to the plaster.
3. Add some water to form a soft dough.
4. Squeeze the plastic bag with the hands to mix the water, paint and plaster. When the plaster feels warm to the touch, it is beginning to set and will set quickly.
5. Hold the bag in any desired shape as the plaster hardens.
6. When the sculpture is hard, remove it from the bag.
7. Paint further with ready-mixed paint, if desired.
8. Glue the sculpture to a wooden block or piece of board for a base, if desired.

HINT *Experiment with the measurements of plaster and water before trying this with young artists. Measurements can vary from day to day, but a half bag of plaster and a quarter cup of water is a good start.*

Frozen balloons

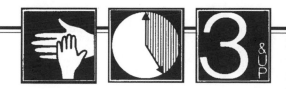

Materials
- balloons, all shapes and sizes
- water
- baking tray
- freezer
- large tub or water table, filled with water
- eyedroppers
- food colouring or watercolour paints

Art process
1. Fill each balloon with water.
2. Place the balloon on a baking tray in the freezer for two days.
3. Remove the balloons from the freezer. Tear and pull away the balloon.
4. Place the frozen ice balloons in a large tub filled with water or in a water table.
5. Drop food colouring or watercolour paints on to the frozen balloons. Push, float and manipulate the balloons into designs and patterns.

Variations
- Drop coloured salty water on the frozen balloons and see what happens.
- Fill the balloons with coloured water before freezing.
- Water can be frozen in many different containers, bags and moulds to add to the floating ice sculpture.
- Fill the balloons with ready-mixed paint thinned with water. "Paint" with the frozen balloons on paper.

HINT — *A group of artists may enjoy standing around the tub of water to watch the colours mix and swirl, and the ice balloons float, sink and bump into each other.*

Eggshell mosaic

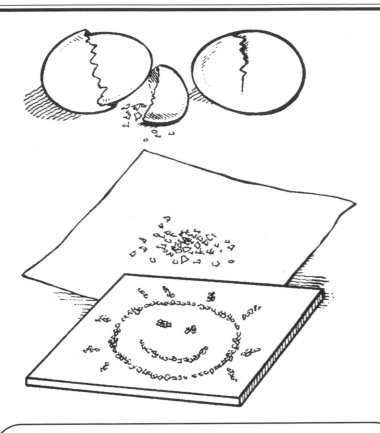

Materials
- dyed eggs, peeled
- greaseproof paper
- rolling pin
- board or cardboard
- glue

Art process
1. Peel dyed eggs such as those used at Easter.
2. Save the shells.
3. Place the shells on greaseproof paper.
4. Crush the shells with a rolling pin.
5. Glue crushed shells on board or cardboard.
6. Dry the project.

Variations
- Colour on the shells of hard-boiled eggs with felt pens instead of dyeing them. Peel these and use for the coloured shells.
- Glue the pieces of egg shell in a definite mosaic pattern on heavy board or paper.
- Use tiny scraps of paper, confetti or paper punch holes in addition to the egg shell.

 HINT
Young children do not always have the coordination or patience to work with picking up tiny pieces of shell. Give them a toothpick or cotton swab to dip first in glue and then touch to the shell piece. A little dot of glue on the paper will help pull the shell off the toothpick or cotton swab and on to the paper.

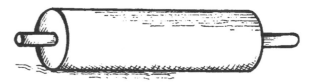

String collage

Materials
- colourful scraps and pieces of wool, embroidery thread or string
- scissors
- liquid starch
- heavy paper
- styrofoam tray
- scissors

Art process
1. Cut the string or wool into 70 cm lengths.
2. Soak the string for a few minutes in a styrofoam tray filled with liquid starch.
3. Place the tray near the edge of the heavy paper.
4. Pull one strand of wool or string out of the tray.
5. Arrange it on the heavy paper in any shape or design.
6. Repeat with many strands of different colours.
7. Dry the string collage overnight.

Variation
- Add this wool to a starch-based finger painting and move the wool around in the painting to form designs.

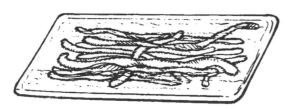

Liquid starch

HINT   Glue can be substituted for the starch, and it works just as well.

COLLAGE

Paper dolls

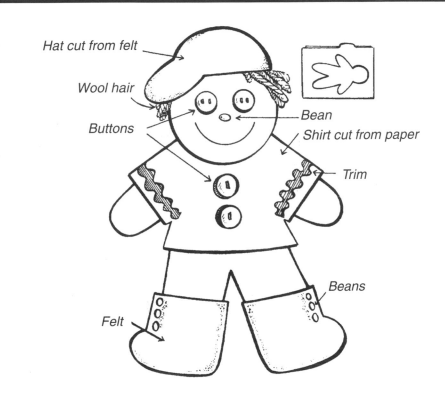

Hat cut from felt

Wool hair

Buttons

Bean

Shirt cut from paper

Trim

Beans

Felt

Materials
- old file folders
- scissors
- glue
- collage items such as wool, buttons, beads, beans, lace or felt
- pens or crayons

Art process
1. **Adult** helps cut old file folders into the shape of a doll body without features or clothing. The shape should be fairly chubby and thick so it will be strong enough to support gluing.
2. Draw or colour on the doll shape before decorating further.
3. Begin decorating the doll shape with collage items for hair, eyes, clothing, jewellery, a hat, glasses or other features to dress the doll.
4. Allow the doll to dry completely.

Variations
- Make characters for a favourite story or play such as the gingerbread boy, a farmer, a farmer's wife and a wolf.
- Make the paper dolls into puppets by taping each one to a dowel or stick so they can be manipulated above a partition or curtain.
- Removable clothing for the doll can be made from paper or fabric scraps.

HINT *Young artists tend to use a lot of glue when adding the collage items, so carry the doll flat to a drying area and leave for a day or two. If the doll is carried upright, all the glue and collage items will slide off the doll shape.*

Neon weave

Materials
- black board (or cardboard painted black)
  cut in 20 cm x 20 cm squares
- bright wools in any lengths (not more than 2 metres)
- tape

Back

Art process
1. Cut slits 1 cm deep around each side of the square. Young children tend to cut the slits VERY close together like the fringe of a scarf. Encourage them to space the slits about 2–4 cm apart for a strong weaving. Spaces can be cut much further apart too. Help as needed.
2. Tape the end of a piece of bright wool to the back of the square and pull it through one of the slits.
3. Cross the wool back and forth over the front of the square, pulling it through the slits to hold. Use slits more than once if needed.
4. When one colour of wool runs out, add new colours of wool by taping the end of the new colour to the back of the square. Continue to wrap, weave, cross and decorate the square.
5. When complete, tape the last end of wool to the back of the square or simply pull the wool through one of the slits.

HINT

For easy wool distribution, roll the wool into a ball and place in a cardboard box with a lid. Punch a hole in the lid and feed the wool through the hole. Place the lid back on the box. Now the wool can be pulled through the lid without tangling. Cut a slit on the edge of the lid. Use this to tuck the loose end of the wool until the next person uses the wool. The box can have many balls of wool and many holes.

CRAFT

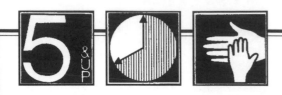

Papier mâché bracelets

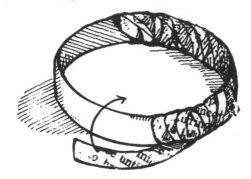

Materials
- cardboard strip about 30 cm long and 1.5–5 cm wide
- wallpaper paste
- newspaper torn into small strips
- about 1.5–5 cm strips of thin white paper (typing paper)
- clear gloss enamel, optional   • liquid starch
- stapler   • felt pens
- ready-mixed paints   • scissors
- coloured tissue paper

Art process
1. Help the artist measure a cardboard strip bracelet around his or her wrist. Leave enough room to fit the artist's hand loosely and allow for thickness added by the papier mâché.
2. Remove the strip from the wrist, overlap the ends and staple.
3. Dip a piece of newspaper into the wallpaper paste and wrap around the bracelet. Repeat this process until the bracelet is covered with at least three layers of the newspaper.
4. Cover the bracelet with strips of thin white paper so that the newsprint will not show through later. The paper will adhere without extra paste.
5. Dry the bracelets for several days.
6. Decorate the bracelet by painting or drawing. Covering the bracelet with liquid starch and pieces of coloured tissue is also pretty.
7. Dry the bracelet again.
8. When dry, an **adult** may paint the bracelet with a clear, glossy paint or polymer to add shine and protect the paint, pen drawings or coloured tissue.

HINT

One effective way to dry the bracelets is to hang the bracelet over a cardboard tube, clothes hanger or clothesline rope.

Young artists may need help starting to wrap the papier mâché around the bracelet strip.

Papier mâché can be a magical wonder to young children. Prepare for being messy and the fun will be worth while.

Bonnets

Materials
- paper plate
- hole punch
- string or elastic
- decorative items such as ribbon, lace, fabric scraps, beads, artificial flowers, bows, felt scraps, streamers, confetti or glitter
- crayons, felt pens or paints
- glue

Art process
1. An **adult** should punch a hole on each side of the paper plate. Tie pieces of string through the holes to make a chin strap to hold the bonnet in place when it is complete.
2. Turn the plate upside down on the table.
3. Begin attaching decorations and collage items to the plate to create a bonnet. Use crayons or pens to further decorate the bonnet.
4. Keep the underside of the hat plain for easier handling. If decorating the underside is desired, have the artist do this before decorating the top of the bonnet.
5. Dry the bonnet thoroughly and then wear it.

Variations
- Play music and have the artists march in a bonnet parade.
- Use only tissue scraps, doilies and foil for a daintier design.
- Create a "theme" bonnet, such as the environment, favourites, pets.

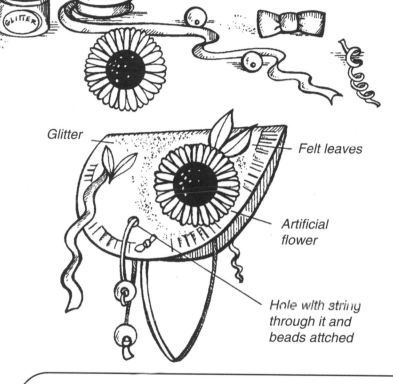

Glitter

Felt leaves

Artificial flower

Hole with string through it and beads attched

HINT

Use one piece of elastic attached to both holes of the bonnet. Measure the elastic from one side of the bonnet, under the child's chin, to the other side of the bonnet. No tying necessary!

CONSTRUCTION

Brushed chalk

Materials
- hammer or other crushing tool such as a rock
- old ends of coloured chalk
- small pie tins
- liquid starch in cups
- paintbrushes
- paper

Art process
1. Place old ends of chalk in pie tins. Gently push the hammer head against the chalk until it crushes. Hold on to the pie tin while crushing. Supervise this activity closely.
2. Place one colour of crushed chalk in each pie tin and mix a rainbow of colours together in another pie tin.
3. Using a paintbrush, paint liquid starch on the sheet of paper in any design or pattern.
4. Pinch bits of chalk powder and sprinkle it on the liquid starch design. The chalk will absorb the starch and become bright and moist.
5. If desired, paint over the chalk and starch design with more starch or add more chalk powder. Experiment with the mixing and painting of chalk powder and starch.
6. When complete, dry the project for about an hour.

Variations
- Mix liquid starch in the pie tin with the crushed chalk until the consistency of paste. Paint with the chalk starch mixture on paper.
- Mix the crushed chalk with PVA glue or sugar water and paint the mixture on paper.

HINT *Artists of any age can crush the chalk with some supervision and encouragement. The magic word is "gently". A rock may work better than a hammer for some children. Any crushing tool is fine as long as it works.*

Marking pen paint

Materials
- water-based marking pens, all colours
- absorbent papers such as paper towels, coffee filters, blotting paper or napkins
- drawing paper
- plastic spray bottle filled with water, nozzle set on spray

Art process
1. Draw freely with marking pens on a variety of papers.
2. Spray the marking pen designs with water and watch the colours blend, blur or separate.

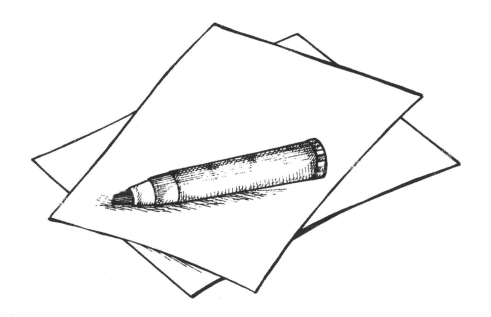

 HINT *Work on a covered surface; wet pen markings can soak through on to the table.*

Most pens are water-based but may not say so. Permanent pens will not work; these pens are always marked "permanent".

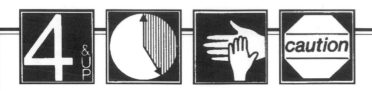

Dig it crayons

DRAWING

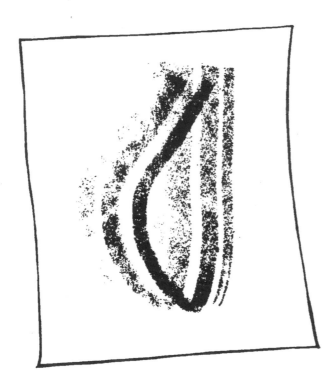

Materials
- jumbo crayons
- tools such as a plastic knife, toothpick or paper-clip
- paper

Art process
1. **Adult** helps the artist cut or dig designs into the sides of the jumbo crayons. Cut wedges, scratch grooves, dig dots and holes or make other shapes. Work on all sides of the crayon. Crayons can break if they are pressed too hard while being carved, but broken pieces can be used for colouring too.
2. Rub and colour with the sides of the crayons. Designs will emerge in the picture due to the shapes and designs cut into the crayons.

Variation
- Make crayon rubbings with the grooved crayons. (See page 20.)

HINT *Artists may need help holding the crayons while they make the designs in the sides of the crayons. One way to assist them is to give the artist a chunk of play clay, flatten it into a rectangle about 2.5 cm thick and press the crayon into the clay. This makes a soft barrier to hold the crayon while carving it and keep it from rolling.*

Towel chalk design

Materials
- heavy paper towels
- saucepan of hot water
- coloured chalk

Art process
1. Place a heavy paper towel in a saucepan of hot water.
2. Remove the towel, and wring it out. Help is needed.
3. Help the artist place the wet towel on a bare table and smooth out the wrinkles by hand.
4. Draw any design on the wet towel with the coloured chalk.

Variations
- Paint on wet paper towels with watercolour paints.
- Drop food colouring or watercolour paints from an eyedropper on the wet towels.

HINT *Towels tear easily if too much pressure is used with the chalk. Have lots of towels ready as artists experiment with drawing in a way that won't tear the towels. Torn towels are perfectly permissible.*

D R A W I N G

DRAWING

Magic drawing

Materials
- cotton swabs
- coloured tissue paper
- liquid bleach
- small bowl
- white paper

Art process
1. **Adult** places about one tablespoon of bleach in a bowl. (Keep the lid on the bleach bottle and keep it out of the reach of children.)
2. Dip the cotton swab into the bleach and draw on the coloured tissue paper to make the colour fade away.

Variation
- Slip a piece of white paper under the tissue paper so that the design is more clearly visible. Experiment with other colours of paper under the coloured tissue paper.

HINT

Bleach requires one-to-one supervision with young children.

Remember bleach can take the colour out of clothing too, so have children wear aprons or play clothes.

Powder painting

Materials
- powdered paint in small pie tins
- paintbrushes
- liquid starch
- paper

Art process
1. Pour a puddle of liquid starch on to the paper.
2. Spread the starch over the paper with a paintbrush.
3. With a different slightly damp paintbrush, dip into the powdered paint and dab it on to the starch-covered paper.
4. The paint will dissolve and become thicker, creating an unusual texture.

HINT

Big, heavy paper such as lining paper works well.

Pie tins can flip over. You may want to use flat styrofoam grocery trays taped to the table when working with younger children.

Golden syrup colour

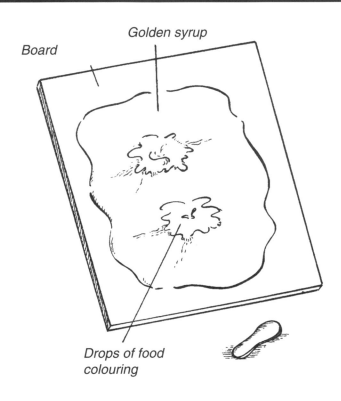

Board

Golden syrup

Drops of food colouring

Materials
- board or cardboard
- food colouring
- golden syrup
- paint aprons
- craft sticks or spoons

Art process
1. Pour a small puddle of golden syrup on the board or cardboard. Spread it out towards the edges with a craft stick or spoon.
2. Squeeze a few drops of food colouring randomly on the golden syrup.
3. Blend the colours in with the fingers.
4. Dry the artwork for several days for a bright, shiny, rainbow coloured design.

Variation
- Use golden syrup colours on an egg-shaped piece of heavy paper for a spring design. You may also choose to make these designs on any shape of paper to complement a theme or festivity.

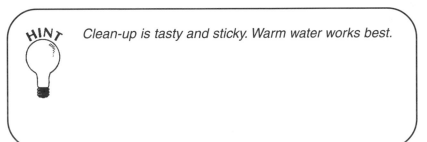

HINT *Clean-up is tasty and sticky. Warm water works best.*

Egg paint

Materials
- 4 egg yolks
- 4 bowls
- food colouring
- paper
- paintbrush

Art process
1. With adult help crack eggs and separate egg yolks. Place one egg yolk into each bowl. Save egg whites for other art ideas.
2. Add a few drops of food colouring to each yolk and mix. Mix red, blue and yellow food colouring to make a new colour in the fourth cup.
3. Paint the bright, glossy colours on the paper.

Variation
- Paint on toast, hot dog buns or biscuits. Warm the food or bake briefly to dry the egg paint.

HINT *Use wide bowls which do not tip easily. Styrofoam grocery trays make great containers for mixing the egg yolk and food colouring.*

Add a few drops of water to tray or cup if paint thickens or begins to dry before painting is complete.

PAINTING

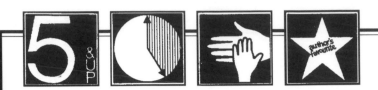

Marbling

Materials
- waterproof inks, variety of colours
- large styrofoam grocery trays
- plastic spoons
- light colour blotting paper
- apron
- newspaper-covered drying area

Art process
1. Fill the grocery trays halfway with water.
2. Gently drop a small amount of waterproof ink on to the surface of the water. Add drops of additional colours.
3. Stir the ink over the water with a plastic spoon slowly and carefully. (The ink will swirl and float forming beautiful patterns.)
4. With **adult** help, place the blotting paper on top of the floating colours for about thirty seconds.
5. With **adult** help, quickly lift off the paper, turn it over and hold it flat to stop the colours from running.
6. Dry the coloured paper on a flat, covered surface. This project can take several days to dry.

Variation
- This project is very pretty to watch using a clear glass bowl with a piece of plain white paper beneath the bowl. Skip the paper printing step and just enjoy watching the colours swirl and mix in the bowl.

HINT

Using small squares of paper makes this project easier to control.

Adult supervision is necessary when working with waterproof ink, both in use and in clean-up

Print relief

Materials
- squares of cardboard or a gift box
- scissors
- glue
- newspaper to cover table
- ready-mixed paint in shallow pan
- paintbrush
- print roller, child's rolling pin or dowel
- paper or cloth

Art process
1. Draw and cut out a design from the cardboard or gift box.
2. Glue the design to a cardboard backing.
3. Place the cardboard design on the newspaper-covered table, design side up.
4. Apply paint over the cardboard design with a paintbrush.
5. Place a piece of fabric or paper over the design.
6. Roll the print roller or rolling pin over the paper or fabric to make a print.
7. Peel the paper or fabric away from the cardboard. The design will transfer to the fabric or paper.
8. Dry the project completely.

Variation
- Brush different colours on to specific parts of the design for a multicoloured print.

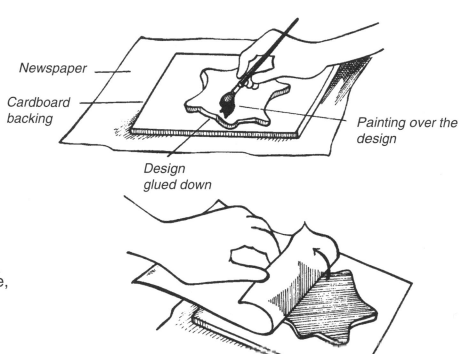

Newspaper

Cardboard backing

Painting over the design

Design glued down

HINT Cutting cardboard is very hard for young artists. Offer help as needed.

Sometimes the paper folds over and sticks to itself when it is peeled from the design. Be sure to use two hands.

PAINTING

Pressed play clay

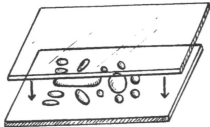

Duct tape

HINT

Be sure the clear plastic is fairly strong and thick (2–3 mm thick) so it won't snap or break during the pressing stage. Lots of helping hands during the pressing will help prevent the plastic from cracking. Using little balls and pinches of clay help, too!

Instead of saving the pressed clay design, the plastic sheets can be peeled apart and the clay can be scraped off and used again.

Materials
- play clay in a variety of colours
- 2 square sheets of clear plastic 25 cm x 25 cm or smaller
- silver duct tape for a frame
- large paper clip for a hook, optional

Art process
1. Place one sheet of clear plastic on the floor.
2. Place little balls and blobs of coloured play clay on the sheet of plastic. Place them at random or in a particular design such as flower shapes. Small bits and pinches of clay work best.
3. Take the second sheet of clear plastic and gently place it on top of the clay design.
4. While kneeling over the project, press the sheet of plastic down with both hands on the clay. Watch the coloured clay squish, spread, flatten and blend together.
5. Twist, rock, or squish if desired.
6. **Adult** secures the two sheets of plastic together with wide silver duct tape. Tape along all four edges to make a silver frame with the play clay design inside.
7. Unbend a large, heavy paper clip. Insert it through the duct tape to create a hook for hanging the clay picture.

Variations
- Place blobs and drops of paint on a piece of paper. Press a sheet of clear plastic on the painted paper and watch the design smear, squish, blur, swirl and blend. Peel off the plastic and a pressed paint design will remain on the paper.

Salt ceramic

Materials
- 200 g of salt
- 100 g of cornflour
- 180 ml of water
- measuring jug
- saucepan
- cooker
- wooden spoon
- piece of aluminium foil

Art process
1. **Adult** cooks the salt, cornflour and water over medium heat. Stir constantly with the wooden spoon until the mixture thickens into a big pure white glob. (One batch of this recipe makes a ball the size of a large orange.)
2. **Adult** removes the mixture from the heat.
3. Place the mixture on a piece of foil until cool.
4. Knead thoroughly until soft and pliable.
5. Sculpt any objects or designs. (See suggestions below.)
6. Embed feathers, toothpicks, pebbles or other embellishments while the ceramic is still soft.
7. This material will dry to a rock hardness without baking.

Variations
- For a shiny sculpture, an **adult** can coat finished dry objects with a clear glaze or fingernail polish.
- Some ideas of things to make include: pendants, beads, figures, letters, holiday decorations, items to glue on plaques, play fruit, play vegetables and play biscuits.

 HINT Cream food colouring or ready-mixed paint can be added to the water if coloured dough is preferred.

This recipe keeps in a plastic bag for a few days. Knead the dough before using to restore softness.

S C U L P T U R E

C R A F T

Bottle bank

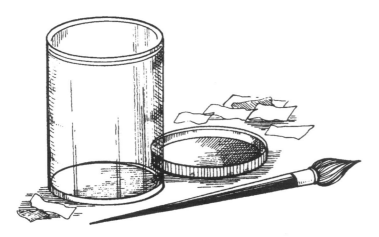

HINT

Smooth out wrinkles in the tissue with the paintbrush.

One layer of tissue should be enough. However, young artists like to pile on several layers of tissue paper. If you like, explain that one layer allows more light to shine through the tissue.

Materials
- glass bottle or jar (with lid)
- small pieces of coloured tissue
- PVA glue thinned with water in small dish
- paintbrush
- table covered with newspaper
- block of wood
- hammer
- screwdriver or chisel

Art process
1. Remove the lid and stand bottle or jar upside down.
2. Paint a little thinned glue on the jar in one area.
3. Press a piece of tissue into the glue and then paint over the tissue piece with more glue.
4. Continue painting areas with glue and adding more tissue to the glue. Overlap pieces so glass does not show through.
5. Be sure to paint down any edges of tissue with the glue. Bring tissue as close to the opening of the bottle as possible. Do not extend the tissue over the edge or inside the bottle.
6. Dry the project. While drying, an **adult** places the lid on a block of wood, right side up to begin making the slotted lid.
7. Place a screwdriver or a chisel point against the lid and hit the handle with a hammer. This will drive the tool through the lid, making an opening. Hammer several more cuts if necessary to make room for 50 pence pieces. Sometimes it is necessary to turn the lid over and pound the sharp edges down with the hammer.
8. Screw the lid on the dry bottle and begin saving money.

Napkin rings

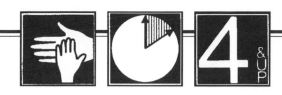

Materials
- cardboard tube (from paper towels)
- knife or scissors
- ready-mixed paints
- brushes
- art tissue paper
- liquid starch
- clear contact paper
- clear gloss enamel, optional

Art process
1. **Adult** cuts the cardboard tube into sections about 5 cm in length with a knife or scissors.
2. Paint the sections or rings with a single colour of paint to coat. Dry. Apply a second coat.
3. Paint designs on the painted sections or attach pieces of art tissue to the rings with liquid starch.
4. Dry the rings.
5. When dry, an **adult** covers each ring with a strip of clear contact paper to protect napkins from paint or tissue stains.

Variations
- Use felt pens to decorate the rings.
- Cover the rings with papier mâché. Paint the rings when dry.
- Instead of using the contact paper, an **adult** coats the rings with clear gloss enamel for a hard, clear finish.

 **HINT**

Use the napkin rings at meals or snacks.

Dry rings on a dowel or bottle tops.

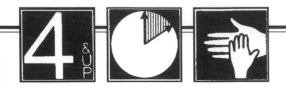

Walking puppets

Drawing glued to old file holder

Holes cut for fingers

Materials
- child's drawing
- scissors
- stiff paper or cardboard
- PVA glue
- fingers

Art process
1. Cut out a drawing and glue it to a piece of stiff paper or cardboard. (Old file folders work well.)
2. With adult help, cut two holes about 6 mm apart at the base of the drawing. Make each hole large enough to let a finger through.
3. Put two fingers through the holes in the puppet. The fingers become the legs of the puppet.

Variations
- Put one puppet on each hand for a show, story or play.
- Several artists can combine their puppets for a show with several characters.

HINT

Any size or any drawing can be a puppet. It is not necessary for the puppet to be an animal or a person. Even a design can be a puppet.

Metal cloth stitchery

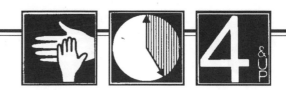

Materials

- 15 cm x 15 cm square of metal cloth (sometimes called hardware cloth, available at hardware stores)
- wool, string or embroidery thread
- blunt, plastic darning needle
- masking tape

Art process

1. **Adult** tapes the edges of the hardware cloth with masking tape to prevent hurt fingers.
2. Using a needle threaded with wool, string or thread, push the needle in and out of the holes. Create any patterns or designs.
3. Add other colours.
4. Tie or tape the wool on the back of the hardware cloth when complete.

Variations

- Other items can be stitched into the design such as old beads, feathers, bits of paper or confetti.
- Pieces of ribbon or lace can be woven through the stitchery if desired.
- A needle is not necessary if the end of the wool is taped with masking tape to resemble a needle.

Tape

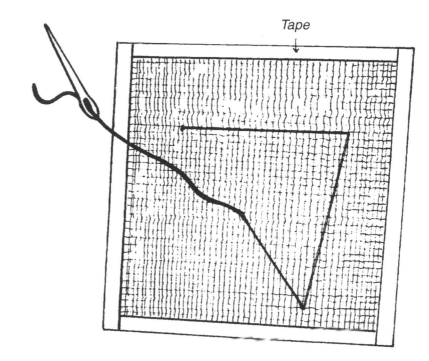

 HINT

Metal cloth is often used for the tops of hamster cages. An alternative is a tapestry screen, which will be more pliable.

Young artists always have difficulty if the wool is too long. An arm's length of wool is a good length to use. An adult should be handy to help change wools or thread needles during the sewing step.

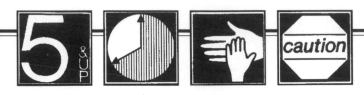

Boiled paper treasure box

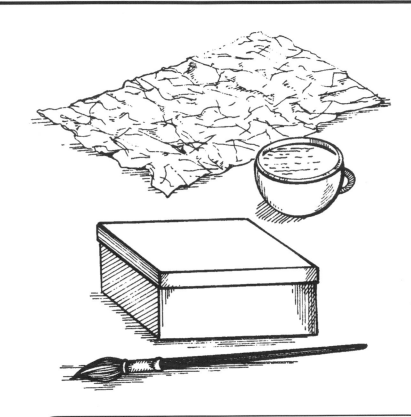

Materials
- wrapping paper or shelf paper
- fabric dye, light colour
- hot water
- saucepan
- cooker
- cardboard jewellery box
- PVA glue in cup
- paintbrush

Art process—boiled paper:
1. **Adult** dissolves the dye in hot water in the saucepan.
2. Crumple up the paper and add it to the dye. **Adult** boils the dye and paper for five minutes.
3. **Adult** rinses the paper in cold water.
4. The artist carefully squeezes out the water from the paper.
5. Spread out the paper to dry on a table or flat surface. The dry paper will look like leather and can be used in any papier mâché project or for the treasure box project.

Art process—treasure box:
1. Turn the box and lid upside down.
2. Paint the box with PVA glue.
3. Cover the box with strips, torn pieces or a large piece of the dry, boiled paper.
4. Place glue on the inside edge of the box.
5. Continue gluing boiled paper over the rim and into the inside of the box. Cover the entire box and lid inside and out. Dry the box.
6. Use this leathery-looking box for treasures.

HINT

The box must be thoroughly dry before placing the lid on top. Sometimes the lid or box edge are so thick that they won't fit back together. Try not to put too much paper on the edge of the box or inside the lid.

Big box sculpture

Materials
- cardboard boxes, all shapes and sizes, such as a shoe box, milk carton, jewellery box, match box, cling film box, paper towel tubes, wine shop box or stationery box
- cardboard tubes
- other paper or cardboard items
- PVA glue
- masking tape
- scissors
- strong wool
- additional collage materials, optional
- thick paints with washing-up liquid added
- paintbrushes

Art process
1. Tape boxes and tubes together to make abstract sculptures. Fit boxes inside one another; bend boxes to make new shapes; cut boxes into new shapes and so on.
2. Use heavy wool to string boxes together to hang the sculpture from the ceiling.
3. Glue any additional collage materials as desired.
4. Paint the cardboard sculpture. Dry overnight.

Variation
- Instead of an abstract sculpture, make animals or space-age cities, cars, rockets, dragons, boats or other inventions or machines.

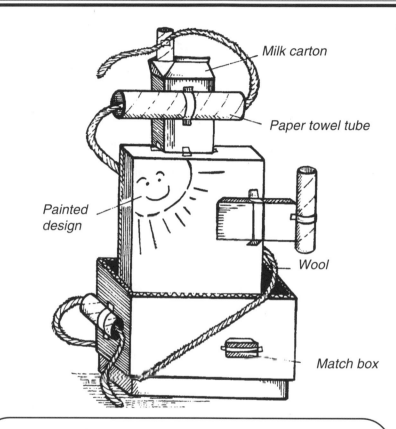

Milk carton

Paper towel tube

Painted design

Wool

Match box

HINT *Adding washing-up liquid to the paint helps it stick to shiny or slick surfaces and helps paint wash out of clothing and come off hands.*

CONSTRUCTION

Collection assemblage

Materials

- collect materials for the assemblage such as coloured wire, punnets, pizza plates, cotton reels, gift boxes, acorns, pipe cleaners, hole punches, egg cartons, tissue rolls or wrapping paper
- PVA glue
- masking tape
- sticky tape
- paper-clips, paper fasteners
- wool, string
- paints and brushes, optional

Art process

1. Build, assemble, glue and otherwise attach any chosen objects to each other in an assemblage design. An assemblage is like a collage but is more three-dimensional and made up of a more diverse selection of material.
2. Use tape, glue, paper-clips or string to attach materials.
3. Dry the project completely.
4. The artist may decorate or paint the project when complete.

Variations

- Decide on one theme to feature in the assemblage such as happiness, spring, robots, space or transportation.
- Use one art medium such as boxes and containers, paper strips, wood scraps or newspaper rolls instead of a large variety of materials.

HINT

A glue gun is a quick-drying alternative to PVA glue. However, it requires extreme caution and continuous adult supervision at all times. The adult should handle the glue gun with the artist pointing out what needs gluing.

Foil treasures

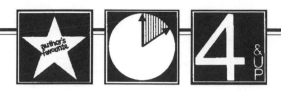

Materials

- small three-dimensional items such as golf tees, rubber bands, paper-clips, buttons, nuts, bolts, washers, beads or pieces of wool
- old paintbrush
- PVA glue
- piece of cardboard
- large sheet of heavy-duty aluminium foil
- tape

Art process

1. Glue any selection of small objects on to a piece of cardboard.
2. Use an old paintbrush to paint PVA glue over the entire surface and all of the objects.
3. Carefully place a large sheet of aluminium foil over the raised surface and glued objects.
4. Gently mould and press the foil around the objects to reveal their shapes. Be careful not to tear the foil.
5. Fold excess foil around the back of the cardboard. Tape or glue it in place.

Variation

- For an antique effect, paint the foil with black paint. Before it dries, wipe the paint off, leaving some paint in the creases and wrinkles.

HINT

Expect the objects to tear through the foil during the first attempts with this project. Later attempts will be more controlled.

Wash the paintbrush thoroughly before the glue dries.

C O N S T R U C T I O N

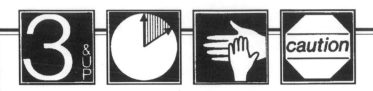

Coffee filter melt

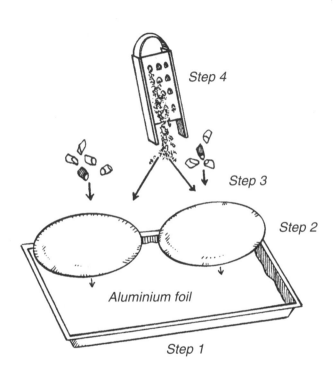

Step 4

Step 3

Step 2

Aluminium foil

Step 1

HINT

Use an old cheese grater that is no longer needed in the kitchen.

Save all crayon stubs. Let the artists peel them.

Materials
- large coffee filters, opened flat
- old crayon stubs without paper, larger crayons
- cheese grater
- aluminium foil
- baking tray
- oven gloves
- wire rack
- warm oven, 200ºF (100 ºC)

Art process
1. Cover the baking tray with aluminium foil.
2. Open and press flat two large coffee filters on the baking tray.
3. Begin dropping little stubs of old, peeled crayons on the coffee filters.
4. Grate some larger crayons into shavings and drop the shavings on the coffee filters.
5. **Adult** places the baking tray in the centre of a warm oven.
6. With an adult watching, leave the door of the oven open to watch the crayon begin to melt and soak into the coffee filter. This usually takes only a few minutes. Or close the oven door and turn on the light so the melting can be viewed from the oven window.
7. **Adult** removes the baking tray from the oven and places it on a wire rack to cool briefly.
8. Remove the coffee filters and hold up to the light to enjoy the colours.

Chalk flowers

Materials

- soft, coloured chalk or pastels
- coloured paper and drawing paper
- blossom shapes cut from old file folders
- facial tissue
- crayons, pencils, felt pens

Art process

1. Place a blossom shape on the coloured paper.
2. Hold the shape with one hand, and with the drawing hand, trace the shape with soft coloured chalk.
3. Without letting go of the shape, take a facial tissue and brush the chalk out and away from the shape.
4. When blended and brushed, remove the shape and see the flower left on the paper.
5. Continue moving and tracing with different colours. Tracings can overlap and touch or be spread out on the paper.

Variations

- Simply trace and draw flower shapes instead of brushing them with the tissue.
- Use different shapes of flowers on one design.
- Colour or paint the traced shapes. Where shapes overlap, make a new colour such as combining red and yellow.
- Use shapes or stencils other than flowers.
- On the same sheet of paper or on a new sheet, trace around the shape with crayon, coloured pencil or felt pen.

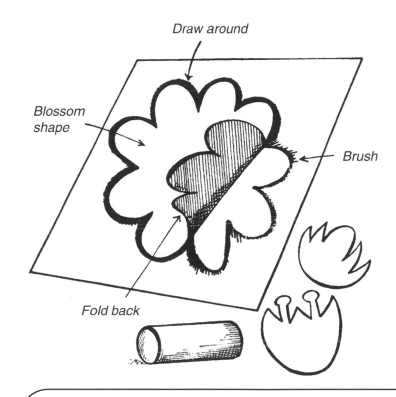

Draw around

Blossom shape

Brush

Fold back

Chalk smudges and blurs are typical to this medium. Expect messy hands and elbows.

One piece of facial tissue should be enough to produce several chalk flowers for each child.

An adult may spray the chalk drawings outside with hairspray or another fixative to reduce smudging.

HINT

D R A W I N G

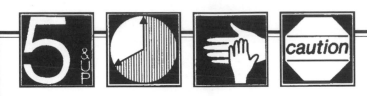

Encaustic prints

Materials
- objects for printing, such as biscuit cutters, plastic toy pieces, rubber stamps, a potato masher, kitchen utensils or cotton swabs
- peeled crayons
- muffin tin, baking tins
- warming tray
- assorted paper

Art process
1. Place one colour of peeled crayon in each cup of a muffin tin. Place additional colours in a baking tin, pie dish or other metal pan.
2. Place the muffin tin on a warming tray and melt crayon until it is liquid (usually no more than ten minutes).
3. With adult help dip gadgets, toys or kitchen utensils into the melted crayon. The melted crayon is HOT: supervise this activity closely.
4. Stamp the item quickly on paper before crayon cools and hardens.
5. Dip the item again and continue stamping.

Variation
- Dip an old paintbrush into the melted crayon and print on paper, stones or wood.

HINT

Encaustic is a term which means "painting with melted wax". It resembles the look of oil painting when a brush is used to paint the wax on paper.

All gadgets, stamps, muffin tins and other printing items will be permanently "crayoned" although they can be washed in hot soapy water with fair results.

Wear old gloves to protect fingers or use clip-style clothespegs to hold gadgets.

Salad spinner

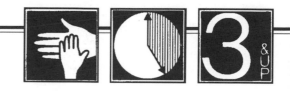

Materials
- plastic salad spinner with lid
- ready-mixed paints in cups
- spoons for each paint colour
- paper
- glitter or confetti, optional

Art process
1. Cut paper to fit into the bottom of the salad spinner.
2. Place paper in the spinner.
3. Drip paint on to the paper with the spoon. Use more than one colour if desired.
4. Snap the lid on the spinner and spin with the handle.
5. Open and add glitter or confetti as desired.

Variation
- Think of other spinning ideas, such as an old record player or a turntable for a game. Experiment with paint, felt pens and crayons.

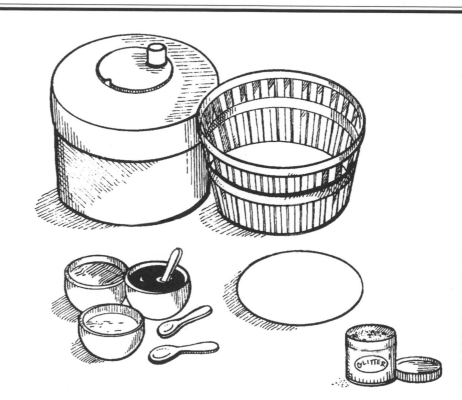

HINT

Younger children may need help spinning.

Prepare a drying area such as newspaper on the floor near the project.

This project is very messy to carry out so have soapy water in a bucket ready for hand washing.

Paint crayons

Materials
- paint crayons
- water in cups
- paper
- paintbrushes, optional

Art process
1. Paint crayons can be found in art and craft shops or from school supply catalogues. They are a water colour base paint in crayon shape.
2. Dip the paint crayon into a small dish of water.
3. Draw with the moistened paint crayon on the paper.
4. Alternatively, use a wet paintbrush to paint on the paint crayon marks, creating additional designs.
5. Dry the painting.

Variations
- Experiment with different textures and colours of papers.
- Make paint crayons by making a thick mixture of powdered paint and water, pour into a muffin tin and dry. Draw with the dry paint like a crayon or dip the dried muffin of paint into a cup of water as described above.

HINT

Be sure to keep water dishes refilled with clean water for the brightest designs. Artists should be encouraged to change their own water.

Do not leave the paint crayons soaking in the dish of water or they will dissolve and disintegrate.

Roller fence painting

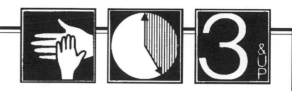

Materials
- outdoor fence
- large trays
- different types of paint rollers
- ready-mixed paint
- large sheets of lining paper
- masking tape
- clean-up materials (bucket, water and cloths)

Art process
1. With masking tape, secure a large sheet of lining paper to an outdoor fence.
2. Fill trays with different colours of ready-mixed paint.
3. Roll paint rollers in trays of paint.
4. Roll paint on the paper.

Variations
- Use a wall or door if a fence is not available. (Cover floor with newspapers.)
- Put textured surfaces under the paper before rolling paint over the paper.
- Do this project on a paint easel instead of a fence.

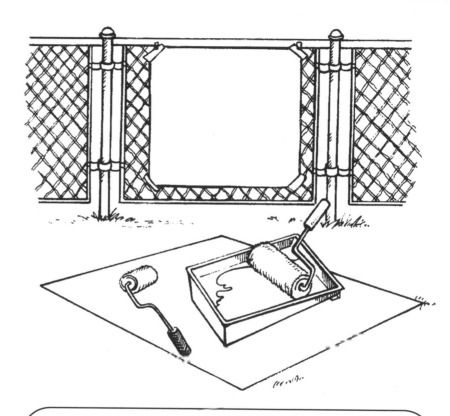

HINT

Do not do this project on the floor or artists will end up crawling through paint.

The fence materials will show through the painting, picking up the textures of wire or wood.

Have clean-up materials handy.

Glitter paint shake

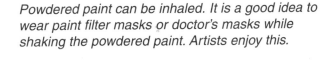

Materials
- board or cardboard
- PVA glue, thinned with water in a cup
- paintbrushes
- salt or cheese shakers with large holes
- powdered paint
- glitter

Art process
1. Paint the entire surface of the board or cardboard with thinned PVA glue.
2. Fill shakers with powdered paint and glitter.
3. Shake the paint glitter mixture on to the glue.
4. Dry the project for a long time.

HINT

Powdered paint can be inhaled. It is a good idea to wear paint filter masks or doctor's masks while shaking the powdered paint. Artists enjoy this.

This project takes a long time to dry, so have a shelf or drying area where it can remain undisturbed for several days.

Salty paint shake

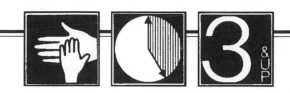

Materials
- bag of table salt
- powdered paints
- containers (margerine or yoghurt)
- PVA glue in small jars
- paintbrushes
- trays
- salt shakers
- paper

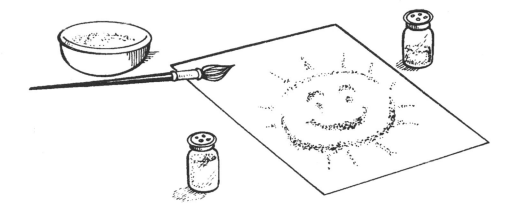

Art process
1. With adult help, mix salt with powdered paint in a container.
2. Put the coloured salt into a salt shaker.
3. Make additional colours for other salt shakers.
4. Paint a design on the paper with a paintbrush dipped in PVA glue.
5. Shake the coloured salt from the shaker on the glue design.
6. Shake excess salt on to the tray to be used again.

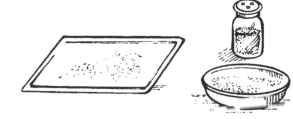

Variation
- Use white beach sand instead of salt. Sand can be purchased in bags from hardware shops or brought home from the seaside or river.

HINT

Some children do better squeezing the PVA glue out of a glue bottle instead of painting it on the paper.

Instead of shakers, younger children may control the coloured salt better when a plastic tub is filled with about 3 cm of coloured sand. The paper is placed in the tub. The artist can use hands to pour sand on the glue design. Pour extra sand back into the tub. This gives a thicker colouration and design.

PAINTING

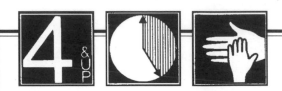

Bubble prints

Materials
- paper
- ready-mixed paint
- liquid detergent
- water
- 500 ml container
- stirring stick or spoon
- shallow aluminium cake tin
- straight straws (not flexible)

Art process
1. The night before the activity, mix one-third cup ready-mixed paint with one-third cup liquid detergent in a 500 ml container .
2. Add water to fill the container and stir.
3. If several colours are desired, make a separate 500 ml solution for each one.
4. Leave the contents sitting overnight.
5. The next day, pour the paint mixture into a shallow cake tin.
6. **Adult** demonstrates how to safely blow through a straw without sucking in. Let the artist press a piece of paper gently on to the bubbles. The bubbles will pop and leave an imprint on the paper.
7. Next, the artist can experiment with bubble blowing and pressing the paper into the bubbles to achieve a bubble print or design.

Variations
- Use various papers for different printing results.
- Instead of paint, blow bubbles in a bowl of detergent and water only. When the bubbles are thick and high, add some drops of food colouring on the bubbles. Slowly lower a paper plate or piece of paper on to the bubbles and a print of the bubbles will be left on the paper.

HINT

Cut a little nick or hole near the blowing end of the straw to help prevent artists from sucking up soapy solution into the mouth.

For lasting, strong bubbles, add a few tablespoons of sugar to the solution.

Playdough beads

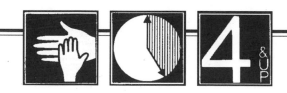

Materials
- 150 g flour
- 100 g cornflour
- 100 g salt
- powdered paint or edible dust (page 27) for colour
- 90 ml warm water
- bowl
- toothpicks
- string, wool or leather strings
- clear gloss enamel, optional

Art process
1. Mix flour, cornflour and salt in a bowl. (Add powdered paint or edible dusting powder for coloured dough.)
2. Add warm water slowly until mixture can be kneaded into a stiff dough.
3. Add flour to reduce stickiness if necessary.
4. Roll dough into balls for beads.
5. Poke a hole in each ball with a toothpick and dry for a few days. (Large beads take longer to dry.)
6. Paint if desired.
7. **Adult** coats the beads with a clear gloss enamel if desired.
8. When the beads are dry, string them on wool, string or leather strips. You may tie knots in between each bead.

Cornflour

Salt

Flour

POWDERED PAINT

Water

HINT

To dry beads, stick toothpicks into a ball of playdough. Place one bead on each toothpick. Twist beads on toothpicks during the drying time to be sure they don't stick to the toothpicks.

This recipe makes a fairly smooth dough that keeps its colour when dry.

A bit of salt residue shows in the beads, especially in darked coloured doughs.

DOUGH

Edible sculpting dough

D O U G H

Materials

- bowl and spoon
- measuring cups and spoons
- 1 teaspoon dry yeast
- 345 ml very warm water
- 1 egg
- 60 ml honey
- 50 g fat
- 1000 g flour
- baking tray
- towel
- 1 teaspoon salt
- 350ºF oven (180 ºC)
- oven gloves

Art process

1. Mix the yeast and very warm water in a bowl.
2. Add the egg, honey, shortening and salt.
3. Slowly add the flour until a ball of dough forms. Add a little more flour if the dough is too sticky.
4. Knead the dough by hand on a floured board.
5. Begin sculpting, making only flat figures as the dough will rise.
6. Cover the sculptures with a towel and put in a warm place for about half an hour to rise. For very puffy sculptures, let the dough rise longer.
7. **Adult** bakes at 350ºF (180 ºC) for twenty minutes or until golden brown.
8. Eat sculptures or save as they are.

Variation

- Insert a paper-clip in the dough before baking and the sculpture will have a hook for displaying. Loop some wool, ribbon or colourful embroidery thread through the paper-clip to hang the sculpture from a tree, nail or doorknob.

HINT

If sculptures sound hollow when tapped with the handle of a table knife, this is a good indication that they are baked and ready to remove from the oven.

Experiment with a garlic press and other tools to make decorations for the sculptures.

Tissue mobile

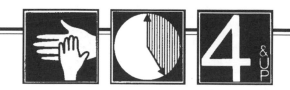

Materials

- wool, 1 metre long
- art tissue or white tissue
- glue mixture in cup—two parts PVA glue to one part liquid starch
- needle and thread
- coat hanger
- watercolour paints, optional

Art process

1. Tie the ends of the length of wool together.
2. Dip the wool in the cup of glue mixture. Run fingers down the wool to squeeze out the excess mixture.
3. Place the sticky wool on a piece of art tissue or white tissue in any shape.
4. Place a second piece of tissue on top of the wool and gently press where the wool touches the tissue.
5. Dry the project overnight.
6. The following day, cut around the outside of the wool shape.
7. Paint on the white tissue with watercolours if desired.
8. Poke a needle and thread through the edge of the tissue next to the inside of the wool.
9. Hang one or many of these shapes from a coat hanger. If the shape was painted, it can dry while hanging.

Variations

- This project makes nice festive ornaments.
- The mobile looks pretty hanging in windows where light can shine through it.

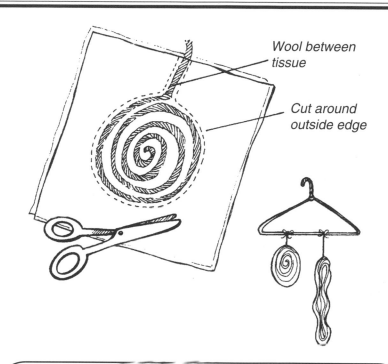

Wool between tissue

Cut around outside edge

SCULPTURE

HINT

When squeezing the excess glue from the wool, pull gently. If pulled too hard, the wool will stretch, spring out of control and flip glue everywhere.

An adult may have to help with placing the second sheet of tissue on the wool and possibly with the cutting step.

An adult should have the needle and thread ready and artists may need help with this step.

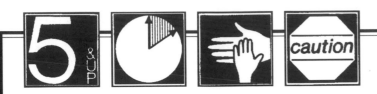

Soap sculpture

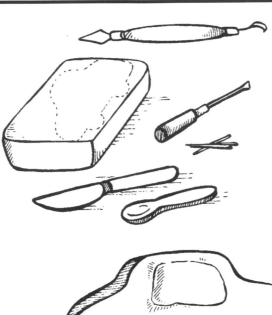

Materials
- bar of soap
- small, fairly sharp knife
- other sculpting tools such as a screwdriver, spoon, toothpick or clay tools
- newspaper

Art process
1. Artists who know how to use a knife safely can do this activity with close adult supervision.
2. Draw the outline of an object on the bar of soap. Select a fairly simple shape without details or intricacies.
3. Use a knife or other tools to sculpt and cut away the soap.
4. To smooth edges of cut sides, rub a wet finger over the spot.
5. Enjoy as a sculpture, or use as a fancy guest soap.

Variation
- See page 47 for the directions of how to make soap balls which can also be moulded or carved.

HINT *Observe caution and supervision with carving. It's a good idea to have a way to brace the sculpture while carving it. For instance, place the soap up against a block of wood which is nailed into another board.*

Sprinkle collage

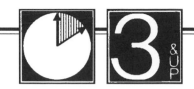

Materials
- PVA glue in squeezy bottle
- paper
- sprinkles such as glitter, confetti, seeds or pine needles
- tray or container for excess sprinkles

Art process
1. Squeeze PVA glue over a piece of paper to make a glue design.
2. Sprinkle the wet glue design with any or all of the sprinkles.
3. Curve the paper and dump excess sprinkles into a container to use for another sprinkle design.
4. Dry the project completely.

Variation
- Other materials for sprinkling include: wood shavings, sawdust, salt, powdered paint, sand or bits of wool.

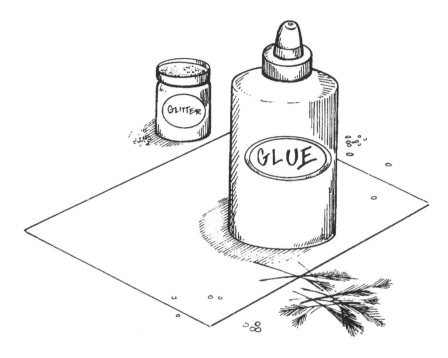

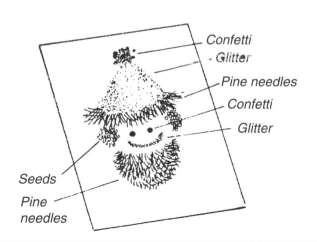

Confetti
Glitter
Pine needles
Confetti
Glitter
Seeds
Pine needles

HINT

Some children can dribble glue from a stick or straw on to the paper better than they can control a squeezy bottle.

Pouring or dumping the excess sprinkles can be tricky, but let the artist try before an adult takes over the job.

Confetti explosion

COLLAGE

Materials
- confetti, paper or metallic
- holes from paper punch
- PVA glue in bottle
- black paper

Art process
1. Draw a design with glue on the black paper.
2. Sprinkle confetti into the glue design. Place confetti and dots one at a time in glue, or sprinkle confetti and dots over the glue all at once.
3. Dry the project completely.

Variations
- Use bits of tissue, cotton wool balls, beads or other collage items instead of confetti.
- Fill a baking pan about 5 cm deep with confetti. Make a glue design on paper, turn the paper over and press the paper into the confetti. Turn right side up and dry.
- Place a glue design in the bottom of a tub of confetti. Scoop confetti over the glue design. Shake off the excess confetti. Dry the project completely.

HINT

Use a damp cotton bud to lift a piece of confetti and place it on the glue design. This makes placing individual pieces of confetti easier than trying to pick them up by hand.

If creating a larger design, work on small parts one at a time, so glue doesn't dry out.

Feeling tree

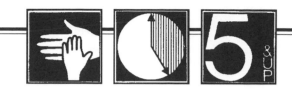

Materials
- fingerpaintings in brown, green or any colours
- paper cake cases
- coloured scraps of paper and tissue
- collage items for a nest such as straw or grass, rolls of newspaper or wool
- scissors
- tape
- glue
- wall or large piece of paper taped to the wall

Art process
1. Cut brown fingerpaintings into sections of a tree trunk and tree branches. Tape them to the wall forming a large tree.
2. Cut green fingerpaintings into leaves and tape them to the brown tree.
3. Add paper cake cases and other scraps of paper for blossom and tape them to the tree.
4. Use collage items to make a nest. For example, little rolls of newspaper resemble sticks. Tape or glue it next to the tree.
5. From scraps of paper, cut out birds, eggs or baby birds and tape in the nest.
6. Add other things to the tree such as caterpillars, butterflies, realistic or imaginary insects ... even a kite!

Variation
- Build a big house and garden with lots of things in the windows, a river filled with fish and boats or under the sea with amazing creatures, plants and fish.

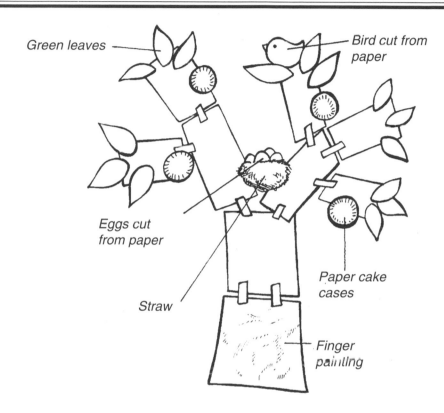

Green leaves

Bird cut from paper

Eggs cut from paper

Paper cake cases

Straw

Finger painting

HINT Collage is an exciting technique for building and creating a picture that can both be seen and felt—a "feeling picture".

Be prepared to see quite unusual things in the tree as young artists have their own perception of trees and nature.

Treasure strings

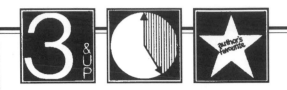

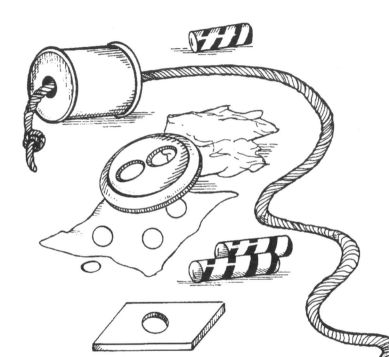

Materials
- heavy wool
- plastic needle
- items for stringing such as sections of tissue rolls, styrofoam pieces, hole-punched paper scraps, foil, egg carton cups, sections of straws, pieces of coloured paper, cotton reels or buttons

Art process
1. Knot the far end of the wool to keep the objects from sliding off. Sometimes it helps to knot one item into the knot to form a barrier to help begin stringing.
2. String any objects on to the wool in a random or a planned pattern.
3. Add more wool if desired to make a very long necklace or a garland to decorate the windows, walls or doorways.
4. Make a necklace, bracelet, belt or hanging.

HINT

Young artists usually need help with threading wool in the plastic needle and with knotting the end of the wool.

If the plastic needle won't go through some papers or items, an adult can make holes with a hole punch, a sharp pencil or scissor point.

Variation
- Plan a theme or specific types of items for the project such as: beads from old jewellery and foil scraps; paper circles and straw pieces; flower shapes and tissue sections; or toys and puzzle pieces.

C R A F T

Fabric notepad

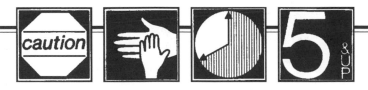

Materials
- inexpensive, small notepad
- rectangular piece of heavy cardboard or thin wood measuring twice as large or more as the note pad
- fabric scraps cut in small squares and other shapes
- scraps of rickrack, lace, ribbon and other notions
- wall hanging hooks
- PVA glue in dish, slightly thinned with water
- PVA glue in bottle
- paintbrush
- small dried flowers, optional
- paper fastener
- piece of string
- pencil
- knife

Art process
1. Glue scraps of fabric all over the piece of cardboard or wood using a brush and the thinned glue. Use plenty of glue. The fabric can be soaked through and will dry nicely later.
2. Glue rickrack, lace or other notions around the border. Dry the project overnight.
3. When dry, glue the note pad to the centre of the decorated cardboard or wood.
4. Glue some dried flowers to the notepad board if desired.
5. **Adult** pokes a hole with a pencil or the point of a knife in the cardboard. Stick a paper fastener through the hole. Wrap one end of string around the paper fastener.
6. **Adult** cuts a groove with a knife into the top end of a pencil and ties the other end of the string around the pencil groove. The pencil will hang on a string next to the notepad, ready to go to work.

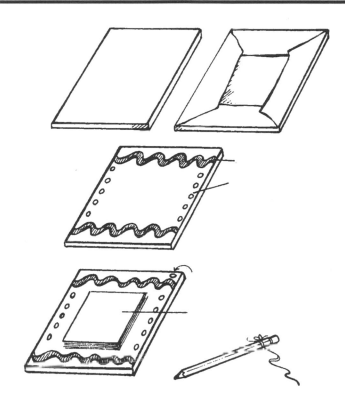

Glue will hold best if allowed to dry completely.

With one-to-one supervision, a glue gun can be used by the adult to glue the artist's work or ideas.

CRAFT

Sea scene

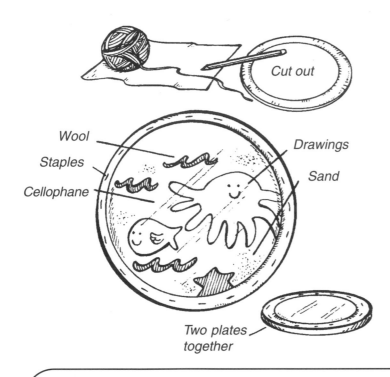

Wool
Staples
Cellophane
Drawings
Sand
Cut out
Two plates together

HINT

The plastic covered rim looks like a window peering into a fish bowl or aquarium.

Artists usually need help controlling the cling film and the stapler.

An adult can use a glue gun for one-to-one help with gluing of the rim to the second plate. As always, observe caution while using a glue gun.

Materials
- two paper plates per artist
- cling film
- felt pens and crayons
- coloured cellophane or art tissue
- scissors
- PVA glue
- wool

Art process
1. With adult help, cut away the centre of one paper plate, leaving the rim.
2. Turn the rim right side up and put glue along the inside edge.
3. Stretch a piece of cling film over the opening and glue it down, creating a window effect. Cut away excess film when dry.
4. Colour and cut out little fish, shells and other sea creatures from the centre piece of the plate.
5. Glue fish, wool, sand, cellophane or tissue on to the second plate.
6. Place the plate rim upside down on the full plate and staple around the outside.
7. Decorate the rim further if desired.

Variation
- Make other scenes on paper plates such as any interesting collage, family portraits, treasure displays or pressed and dried flowers.

CONSTRUCTION

Summer

D R A W I N G

Sand drawing

Materials
- trip to seaside, river or large sandy area (an earthen-floored playground also works)
- bare feet, fingers
- long stick, other drawing tools
- water in bucket or from hose, optional

Art process
1. Go to a large, open sandy beach or earthen-floored play area.
2. Remove shoes and socks.
3. Begin making marks in the sand or earth by scooting and shuffling bare feet through the sand or earth. Use fingers, hands, shells, a long stick or other tools to draw in the sand or earth.
4. If the sand or earth is too dry for a clear impression, add water and moisten the drawing area. Then begin to draw in the moistened sand or earth.
5. Leave the drawing when complete or smooth the earth or sand with a leafy branch, hands or even a broom.

Variations
- Make a footprint trail for others to follow.
- Write names or messages in the sand or earth.
- Add sculpture items such as stones or leaves collected from the surrounding area to enhance the drawing.

HINT

Have towels on hand to clean sandy toes before putting shoes back on.

Be prepared for sandy hands and artists who want to paddle in the water.

Shadow drawing

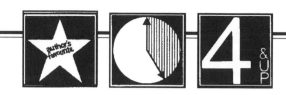

Materials
- large sheet of lining paper
- felt pens, paints and brushes, crayon or chalk
- sunny day outside
- 4 stones, optional

Art process
1. Go for a walk looking for shadows on the ground.
2. Find a shadow that is appealing in design.
3. Place the large sheet of lining paper on the shadow. Adjust the paper so that the shadow is captured on the paper.
4. If the day is windy, place a stone on each corner of the paper to keep it from blowing away.
5. Using any choice of drawing or painting tools, trace, outline, colour in or decorate the paper using the shadow as the design.
6. When complete, remove the paper and observe the shadow drawing.

Variations
- Cut the design out and glue it on another sheet of paper contrasting in colour. Black is often an effective choice for a background.
- Make a shadow drawing of a friend's shadow.
- When using crayon, place textured surfaces behind the paper to add design to the shadow drawing. A wire mesh screen, sheet of plywood, bumpy scrap of vinyl flooring or scrap of formica make interesting textures.

DRAWING

HINT
Crayons take a long time on this design activity, but some children enjoy this. Children also tend to poke holes in the paper so it helps to have cardboard or a sheet of plywood under the paper as a hard surface.

Paint covers fastest. Carry cups of paints and paint brushes in a flat cardboard box to prevent spilling.

Big blot

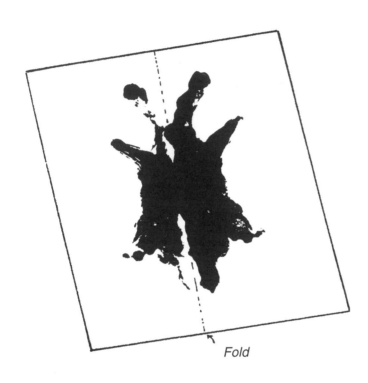

Fold

Materials
- big sheet of lining paper
- spoon or large paintbrush
- ready-mixed paints in containers

Art process
1. Fold paper in half. Open it.
2. Spoon or brush paints mainly on the fold line.
3. Refold and press the paper out from the fold to the edge to move and mix the paints.
4. Open the painting.
5. Carry the big blot to a drying area where the painting can dry flat on newspapers. Dry it completely.

Variation
- When the big blot is dry, some children enjoy cutting out the big blot shape. This can be displayed as they are or glued to another backing in a complementary colour.

 HINT *Younger children will need the paper pre-folded and may need assistance with unfolding the large paper.*

The main appeal of this art experience is the size of the blot. It might help children if they make the traditional small blot on smaller folded paper first so they understand the concept of what they are making.

Fence mural

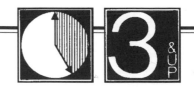

Materials
- long fence
- roll of wide, heavy paper
- tape
- stapler
- paint mixed in cans or wide bowls
- paintbrushes
- small tables, chairs or boxes, optional
- bucket of soapy water and cloths for clean-up

Art process
1. Tape or staple a long, wide, heavy roll of paper to a fence. Use lots of tape or staples so the paper will not tear and fall down.
2. Place containers of paints and brushes at intervals along the fence. To keep paints from spilling, small tables, flat chairs or strong cardboard boxes work well as paint stands
3. Several artists can paint at the same time on the same long piece of paper.

Variations
- Make up a play and use the mural for a backdrop or scenery. Layer several murals which can be changed for different scenes.
- A group of artists could agree on a theme and paint a scene together. Some suggestions are: houses in our neighbourhood, dinosaur world, wild and bright colours, around the world, summer fun or the world's biggest painting.

HINT

Free roll-ends of heavy paper are often available from newspaper printers.

Fence murals make great group or party activities.

Paint will drip down the paper using this method. To improve results mix paints fairly thick and add liquid starch for smoothness.

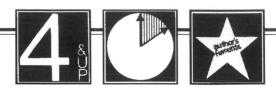

Flicker paint

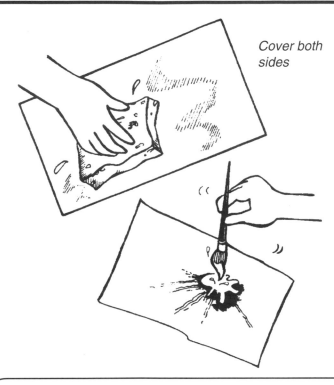

Cover both sides

Materials
- white drawing paper
- water
- sponge
- watercolour paints
- paintbrush

Art process
1. Cover both sides of white drawing paper with a water-filled sponge.
2. Fill paintbrush with watercolour paint and drip drops of paint on the paper.
3. Flick or shake the paint on the paper too.
4. Continue painting this way with other colours.
5. Colours will blend and mix on the wet paper.
6. Let paintings dry in place rather than moving them inside.

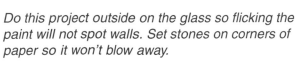

HINT

Do this project outside on the glass so flicking the paint will not spot walls. Set stones on corners of paper so it won't blow away.

Wear old clothes or cover clothing with a big shirt with sleeves cut off to elbow length.

Have a soapy bucket of water handy for cleaning up faces and hands.

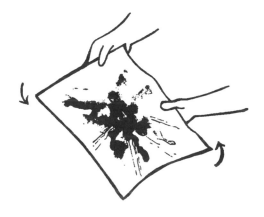

Spray painting

Materials
- heavy white paper
- ready-mixed paints (medium consistency)
- paintbrushes
- spray bottle filled with water (set on spray, not stream)

Art process
1. Place the heavy white paper outdoors on a flat surface such as the grass or inside on a covered floor.
2. Drip paint from brushes on to the paper.
3. Spray clear water from the spray bottle on the drops of paint.
4. Paint drops will thin, spread and mix.

Variation
- Sprinkle powdered paint on heavy paper and spray with water. Do this project on a rainy day and carry outside into the rain to moisten.

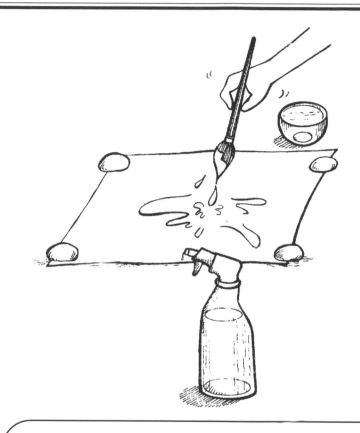

HINT *This is a good outdoor project which leaves plenty of room to "spray".*

Try hanging the paper on a fence so that all the paint runs down. Dry the project on the fence before removing.

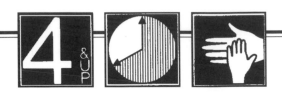

New clay explore

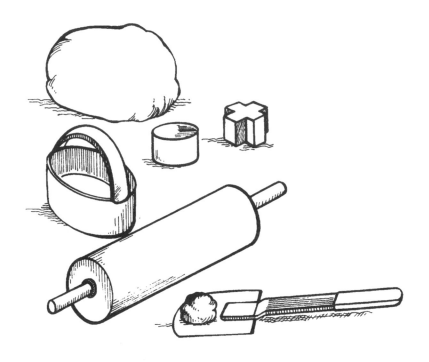

Materials
- new clay, sometimes called moist clay (available from craft shops, art supply shops and school supply catalogues)
- tools such as biscuit cutters, garlic press, knives, nails, toy pieces, a spatula, rolling pin, blocks or toothpicks
- table covered with a heavy-duty rubbish bag
- tape
- covered artist

Art process
1. Protect the work area with a heavy-duty rubbish bag taped down to the table.
2. Roll, squeeze, pound, press and form new clay in any manner desired.
3. Dry the clay objects if the artist wishes to save the work. If not, return the clay to the airtight container to use again later.

 HINT

Store the clay in an airtight container.

Clay can clog drains, so do not wash it down the sink. Use a bucket or bowl of water for washing hands and utensils. Discard the water outside.

This is a messy activity, but a very rewarding and artistically satisfying project.

New clay sculpture

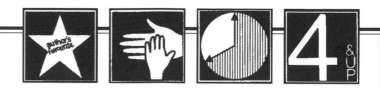

Materials

- new clay, sometimes called moist clay (available from craft shops, art supply shops and school supply catalogues)
- rolling pin or cylinder block
- other tools including a spatula, nails, biscuit cutters, garlic press or knives
- ready-mixed paints
- paintbrushes
- clear gloss enamel or lacquer, optional

Art process

1. Roll out a small portion of new clay about 1 cm thick.
2. Cut out any shape such as a fish, a circle, a square, a heart or a leaf.
3. Decorate the shape with designs pressed or cut into the clay.
4. Dry the clay.
5. Paint designs on to the clay shape.
6. When dry, an **adult** can paint the clay shape with clear gloss enamel or lacquer.

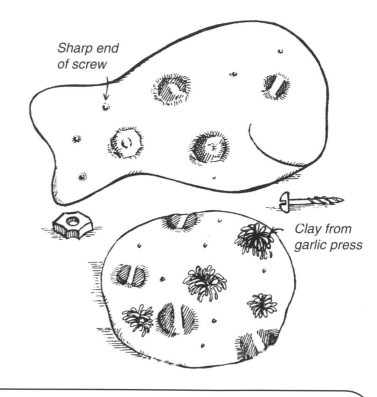

Sharp end of screw

Clay from garlic press

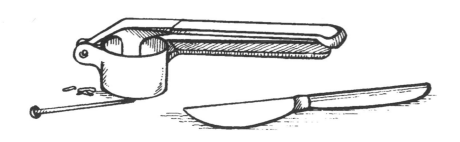

HINT

Protect the work area with a heavy-duty rubbish bag taped down to the table.

Store clay in an airtight container.

Clay can clog drains, so do not wash it down the sink. Use a bucket or bowl of water for washing hands and utensils. Discard the water outside.

Bowling

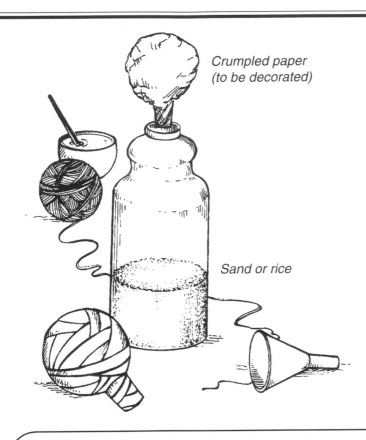

Crumpled paper
(to be decorated)

Sand or rice

HINT *Keep in mid that the bottles can lose their "heads", the paint may chip off or other disasters may occur if the children throw too hard or the alley is too long. Start small for the bowling and realize that most children will naturally overdo the throwing.*

Materials
- plastic juice bottles
- double sheet of newspaper for each bottle
- sand or rice
- funnel
- newspaper torn in strips
- wallpaper paste
- wool
- paint
- paintbrushes
- PVA glue
- collage materials
- clear gloss enamel or polymer

Art process
1. Crumple a double sheet of newspaper into a round shape to make a head on a bottle. Pull out a section for the neck to stick into the bottle.
2. Fill each plastic bottle about one-third full with sand or rice using the funnel. (This will keep bottles from tipping over too easily.)
3. Paste newspaper strips all over the head and down on to the neck of the bottle and all over the entire bottle if desired. Dry the project for several days.
4. Paint decorations on the bottles such as eyes, a nose and a mouth. Add wool for hair. The artist may also choose to paint the bottle using bright colours, shapes and designs. Decorate with collage materials if desired. Dry the project completely.
5. **Adult** paints the bowling bottle with clear gloss enamel or polymer. Dry again.
6. To bowl, set up the bottles at the end of a room. Mark off the floor with masking tape for an alley. Roll soft balls or any other balls down the alley and see how many bottles can be knocked down.

Fence weaving

Materials
- fence (chain link fences work well)
- items for weaving such as crepe paper, strips of fabric, rope, ribbon, lace, strips of newsprint, other paper or wool

Art process
1. Find a fence that is comfortable to reach and easy to stand beside.
2. Weave and wrap materials through the fence.
3. Continue adding decorations and weaving until the fence is woven and decorated as desired.
4. Remove the weaving before it rains, but enjoy it as long as possible.

Variations
- Make a swing-set or playground equipment weaving.
- Plan the fence weaving as part of a party, play or special event.

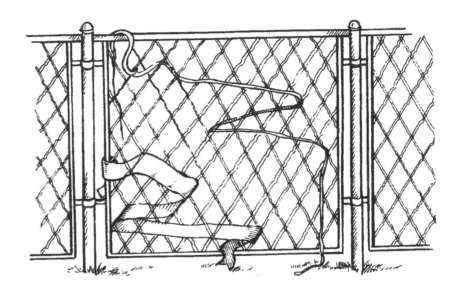

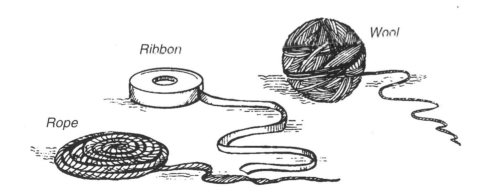

Ribbon

Wool

Rope

HINT
One trick to making weaving easier for young artists is to keep the strips fairly short (not more than 60–100 cm in length).

Another more challenging weaving approach is to roll the strips in a ball and place them in a container with a hole at the top. The artist feeds the strips through the fence wire, unrolling it from the container.

SCULPTURE

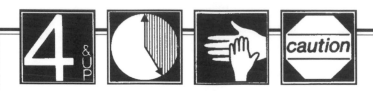

caution

Brick making

Materials
- soil
- water
- plastic bucket
- muffin tins or ice cube trays
- several sheets of newsprint

Art process
1. Put soil in a plastic bucket and mix in just enough water to form a mud ball.
2. Press the mud into muffin tin cups or ice cube tray sections.
3. Place the tins or trays in a warm place for about ten days, or **adult** bakes at 250ºF (130 ºC) for fifteen minutes.
4. When cool, drop the "bricks" on newsprint on the floor and see which ones break and which ones hold together. Use the solid bricks for building.
5. Make as many bricks as possible for the most fun in building.

HINT

Add a little plaster of Paris to the mud mixture so it will hold together better. Experiment with a measurement that works for you as there is no set amount of plaster that works all the time.

Follow the building suggestions for "brick building" (page 245).

S C U L P T U R E

Brick building

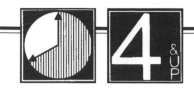

Materials
- homemade soil bricks (see "Brick making", page 244)
- stones or gravel
- sticks and weeds
- plaster of Paris or mud

Art process
1. Attach bricks and other items together in a free-form building using plaster of Paris mixed to a runny consistency for the "cement". Mud also works to stick the items together.
2. Dip, paint or spoon plaster over the items and add them to the building.
3. Dry the project overnight or longer.

Variations
- Build with wood scraps and glue.
- Build with sugar cubes and royal icing (page 127).

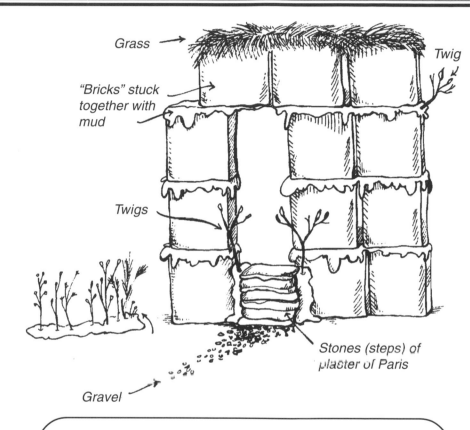

Grass

Twig

"Bricks" stuck together with mud

Twigs

Stones (steps) of plaster of Paris

Gravel

HINT

Keep a soap bucket and towels nearby for clean-up.

Some children really do not like to get their hands dirty. Sometimes this is merely a stage. Be understanding. This project is not for everyone.

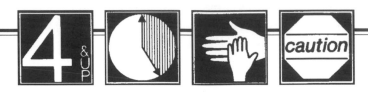
Basket stitching

C R A F T

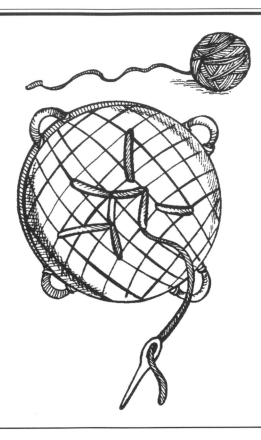

Materials
- loosely woven small cane basket
- wools in many colours
- plastic darning needles
- scissors

Art process
1. Thread a darning needle with a fairly long piece of wool. Use double wool tied at one end for younger children.
2. Begin stitching the wool through the holes in the basket in any random or planned design. Be very cautious of space between artists so no one gets poked with a needle.
3. Change colours as desired.

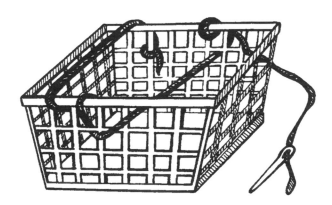

HINT

The firmness of the basket makes it easy for young children to hold and push the needle through the basket.

Children always seem to need help with threading, tying and sometimes starting or ending the stitching.

Pressed flower frames

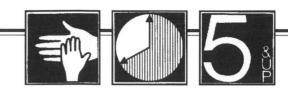

Materials
- fresh flowers
- newspapers
- heavy books
- glue in squeezy bottle
- scissors
- pen
- wooden curtain rings
- heavy paper
- scrap paper
- PVA glue in dish
- toothpicks to dip in glue

Art process

Drying
Place fresh flowers on the newspaper. Flowers should not be touching each other. Put several layers of newspaper on top of the flowers. Lay heavy books on top of the newspaper and flowers. (Bricks or other heavy objects also work well.) Leave the flowers undisturbed for about four weeks to dry completely. (Thick flowers will take longer.)

Framing
1. Place a curtain ring on a piece of paper and draw around the outside of the ring. Cut the circle a little smaller than the drawn circle.
2. Choose a pressed flower and turn it upside down on the circle of paper. Dip the end of the toothpick into the glue and dot it lightly to the back of the flower. Carefully lift the flower and place it glue side down on the paper circle. Repeat until the desired flower design is complete.
3. Apply glue to the back of the curtain ring from a squeezy bottle. Lift the ring and stick it to the paper circle containing the flowers. Keep the screw eye of the ring at the top. Dry the project completely.
4. The ring becomes a frame for the flower arrangement, and the screw eye can be used as a wall hook.

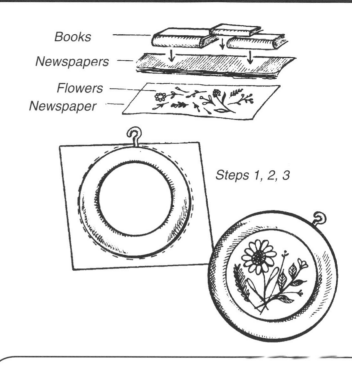

Books
Newspapers
Flowers
Newspaper

Steps 1, 2, 3

HINT

Pressed and dried flowers are delicate and need to be handled with care.

Press flowers a month ahead of time so they are ready for this project.

Young artists can do this project on their own, but assistance is likely to be necessary with the gluing of the ring to the paper. Even if this project doesn't turn out "adult-like", allow creativity to move at the child's pace.

Parade

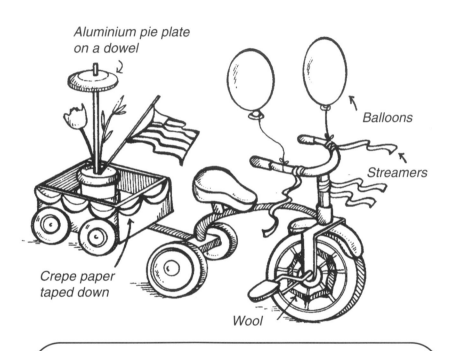

Aluminium pie plate on a dowel

Crepe paper taped down

Wool

Balloons

Streamers

HINT

Expect enthusiasm and noise as part of the fun.

Some children have no concept of staying in line or "following the leader" in a parade setting. Stage a brief practice time before decorating. This will help alleviate confusion later. Straight lines are not important, but a parade needs some form. The artists can decide how they wish the parade to form and proceed.

Materials
- tricycles, bikes, big wheels, scooters or wagons
- decorating materials including crepe paper, balloons, tin cans, aluminium pie plates, flags, streamers, wool and string
- masking tape

Art process
1. Decorate tricycles or other riding or pulling toys for a parade.
2. Some decorating ideas are:
   - weave crepe paper through bicycle spokes
   - tie balloons or streamers to handle bars
   - make a float in a wagon
   - hang noisy cans or pie plates from bikes
3. Start a parade around the playground, park or along the neighbourhood pavements.
4. Add marching people (decorate them too!), rhythm instruments or noise makers to the parade.

Variations
- Parades can have a festive or celebration theme.
- Invite pets to join the parade.
- March to music from a tape recorder.

Boats

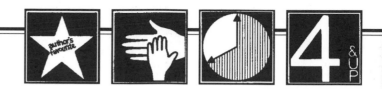

Materials

- boats made from any of the following—milk cartons, match boxes, plastic take-out food containers or styrofoam blocks
- boat decorating and building items including—paper, stick-on reinforcements for paper, clear contact paper, plastic bags, foil, drinking straws, craft sticks, cotton wool balls for smoke, toothpicks or kebab skewers
- PVA glue, masking tape, rubber bands or staples
- water to float boats
- string to pull boats

Art process

1. Begin with a main form to use as the base of the boat such as a milk carton.
2. Attach parts to the boat using tape, glue, staples or other creative ideas. Decorate the boat too.
3. Go to a source of water such as a puddle, pond, children's plastic paddling pool or quiet stream.
4. Attach a string to the boat and launch the boat. Pull the boat as desired.

Variations

- Name the boats.
- Have a boat show or Boats Afloat Celebration.
- Push the boat along with a stick instead of a string.

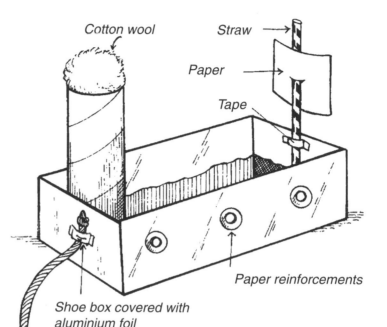

Cotton wool

Straw

Paper

Tape

Paper reinforcements

Shoe box covered with aluminium foil

Wool pull attached with tape and staples

HINT Some boats will not float too well so young artists may wish to test their boats in the sink, make adjustments and launch their boat after sufficient testing.

Masking tape holds very well even when wet; cellophane tape does not.

Stick wrapping

Materials

- 1 metre stick or 1.5–2 cm dowel
- many colours and lengths of wool, string, ribbon or streamers, embroidery thread, fabric strips and other string-like materials
- decorations such as feathers, felt, foil or flowers with stems
- glue
- masking tape

Art process

1. Start wrapping the stick with wool. With adult help, tie a half-hitch knot at the beginning or use masking tape to attach the wool securely to the stick.
2. Continue wrapping the chosen material tightly around the stick.
3. Change colours at any time. The new wool can either be tied to the previous piece of wool or taped to the stick. Begin to wrap the stick with the new colour, texture or material. Loose ends can be left hanging or neatly tucked in. Encourage creativity.
4. As wrapping continues, other decorative items can be tied, taped, glued or wrapped into the wool or string. This gives the wrapping a "surprise" character that makes it unique.
5. Loose ends can also be decorated with any interesting items.

Variation

- Find a pole, pillar or column to wrap with larger strips of fabric, coloured ropes and wool for a large rendition of the wrapped stick.

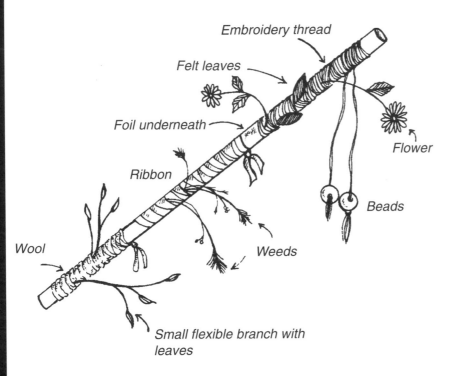

Embroidery thread

Felt leaves

Foil underneath

Flower

Ribbon

Beads

Wool

Weeds

Small flexible branch with leaves

HINT

Wrapping tightly can be difficult for some artists. Use lots of tape or tying to help attach the wool to the stick.

Shorter sticks work well for younger children. Working in pairs can be helpful also: one artist wraps the stick while the second person holds the stick.

C O N S T R U C T I O N

Paper bag kite

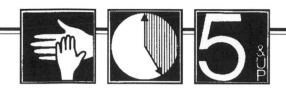

Materials
- large paper shopping bag
- string
- stick-on paper reinforcements
- hole punch
- paints and brushes
- PVA glue
- paper scraps and collage materials
- tissue paper
- crepe paper
- streamers
- ribbons
- paper cake cases

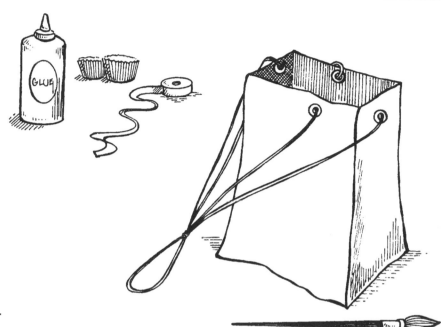

Art process
1. Punch four holes in the paper bag, one on each of the four corners about 1–1.5 cm from the edge of the bag.
2. Stick a reinforcement circle on each hole.
3. Cut two pieces of string to about 1 metre in length. Tie each end of one string into a reinforced hole to form a loop. Make a loop with the second string.
4. Cut another piece of string about 1 metre long. Put it through the two loops and tie it. (This will be the kite handle.)
5. Paint the bag as desired. Allow the paint to completely dry.
6. Glue paper collage materials and streamers to the paper bag kite. Dry the kite completely.
7. Open the bag. Hold on to the string and run. The wind will catch in the bag and the kite will fly out and above the artist.

HINT

For the strongest and most successful kite experience, the bag must dry completely before painting, decorating and flying.

Adult assistance is needed when tying the string to the bag but the decorating and flying is completely child-centred.

Add extra reinforcements or clear contact paper to the holes to make the kite last longer.

CONSTRUCTION

Box car

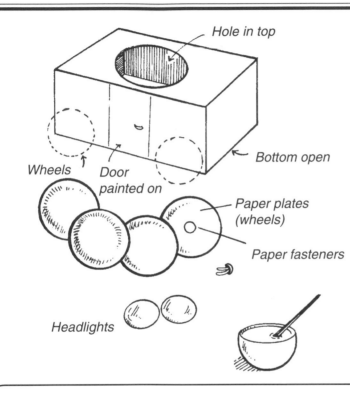

Hole in top

Bottom open

Wheels

Door painted on

Paper plates (wheels)

Paper fasteners

Headlights

Materials
- large cardboard box with top, flaps cut off
- ready-mixed paint, paintbrushes
- paper plates
- heavy string
- aluminium foil
- paper fasteners
- stapler
- tape
- scissors
- felt pens

Art process
1. **Adult** cuts a hole in the bottom of the box large enough to fit over a child's hips.
2. Turn the box over so the hole is on top.
3. Paint the box using any designs. Allow the paint to dry.
4. **Adult** pokes four holes in the box with scissors for the car wheels.
5. To make wheels, push paper fasteners through paper plates and attach them to the holes in the box. Paint the wheels or decorate with felt pens if desired.
6. To make headlights, cover paper plates with aluminium foil. Attach the headlights to the box with tape or paper fasteners. Tape over pointed ends of fasteners inside the box.
7. **Adult** pokes a hole with scissors on either side of the top centre of the box. Thread a heavy string or cord through one hole. Tie a double knot so it cannot slip through the hole.
8. After the young artist steps into the box car, pull it up to the waist. **Adult** pulls the string around the back of the child's neck and over to the second hole. Tie another double knot. Now the car "hangs" from the child's shoulders. The car is ready to "drive".

HINT

This project involves a lot of work, but the fun is worth the work. Let the children do as much for themselves as they can. Tying the string and poking holes in the cardboard is the most difficult part of the project and requires adult help.

Be sure the box dries completely before using as a car. The paint will still tend to smudge off on damp or sweaty hands at play.

CONSTRUCTION

Project index

Materials index

Art medium index